DO I REALLY HAVE TO READ THIS?

A Man's Guide to a Healthy Relationship

Richard Caplan MSW, MPH

authorHOUSE®

AuthorHouse™
1663 Liberty Drive
Bloomington, IN 47403
www.authorhouse.com
Phone: 1-800-839-8640

First published by AuthorHouse   12/14/2009

ISBN: 978-1-4490-3520-4 (e)
ISBN: 978-1-4490-3521-1 (sc)
ISBN: 978-1-4490-3522-8 (hc)

Library of Congress Control Number: 2009910895

Printed in the United States of America
Bloomington, Indiana

This book is printed on acid-free paper.

Contents

PREFACE

If you are a woman reading this book it is because your best friend, mother, sister, or some other woman gave you this and said, "Your man should read this."

If you are a man reading this, it is because your woman gave it to you and said, "Here, you need to read this."

By the way, guys, if your woman did give this to you to read it is because: You're not listening, you're not talking or you don't understand.

INTRODUCTION

I have been a licensed social worker since 1984. During that time I have worked with hundreds of people and many, many couples in various stages of distress. All the information gathered in this book is based on the work I have done with these couples and what they have taught me about how to have a successful or unsuccessful relationship. I also understand that my comments do not describe ALL men and women.

There are men out there who are actually compassionate, attentive and giving people with the capacity for profound levels of intimacy. This book is not for them. This book is primarily for the average guy who has found himself in a situation he is not prepared for nor did he anticipate. He was caught totally off guard and now finds that he has to develop skills that he never dreamed of.

Gentlemen, this book is for you and the women who want to bring you into the twenty-first century.

I will be referencing "men" and "women" as part of a committed relationship but I do not mean to exclude same sex relationships whose problems end up looking strikingly similar to those who are in opposite sex relationships.

Good Luck.

ASSUMPTIONS

Men, we have to face the truth that we are not equipped to have an intimate relationship with anything more complicated than our cars. We have brought women into our lives not only because they are soft and sexy and smell better then we do, but also because on some deep and yet to be discovered level, we recognize the need for emotional connectedness (and not just with our favorite brand of beer).

So please consider this a "how to" book, as in "how to be happily coupled". For in the end, I think you will find that old adage to be true, "A happy woman means a happy man." Or, as that T-shirt saying goes, "If mama ain't happy, ain't nobody happy!"

BASIC PREMISES

To get the full appreciation of this book, there are several basic premises that must be accepted as truth. Without their total acceptance you mught as well put this book down and pick up something about auto mechanics or tools.

BASIC PREMISE #1
Women are all knowing and all wise.
Men are dogs.

BASIC PREMISE #2
Women have an uncanny ability to look into the future and instinctively know the direction their relationship is taking.
Men can't find the paper towels without asking for help.

BASIC PREMISE #3
Women are insightful communicators able to reach an astonishing depth of feeling and sensitivity.
Men can barely grunt.

BASIC PREMISE #4
Women are able to manage, nurture and maintain intimate relationships throughout their life span.
Men's closest relationship is with the television set.

BASIC PREMISE #5
Women notice everything about their man. They know their looks, their expressions and inflections. They know more about their man then their man knows about himself.

If pushed, a man might be able to recall the color of his woman's eyes (but I wouldn't put money on it).

MISSION STATEMENT

A WOMAN'S MISSION
To take her man and have him fulfill his potential whether he wants to or not.

A MAN'S MISSION
To let her.

THE COUPLED MAN'S CREED

Yea, though I am a lowly man, I will strive to reach the great horizon that my woman has directed me toward. And if I fail in that pursuit, it is due to my own limitations as a man and not because my woman has directed me toward the wrong horizon.

CHAPTER 1

IN THE BEGINNING

Women fall in love with the little boy that lives inside of each man. This is where women find the child that they wish to nurture (at least until they have a real child, but more on that later). Once they've established connection with the child, they then get busy looking for the man who surrounds him. This is extremely important for a woman because, in my experience, a woman cannot love a man she doesn't respect.

If, while looking for the man, a woman finds an adolescent boy, then things are not destined to work out well. A woman might still marry this man thinking that she will change him (woman's problem #1) but she will soon learn that an adolescent man remains an adolescent man until he is forced by some force of nature to change.

Men, fall in love with what is in front of them. Consciously, they are not looking for anything more complicated than that.

The old adage is very true: Women fall in love with a man believing he will change. Men fall in love with a woman believing she will not.

CHAPTER 2

COMMUNICATION

The best place to start in any relationship is with communication. Without effective communication, nothing can be resolved, and I am certain there are always things that need to be resolved.

As you most likely know, and will read more about in the next chapter, there are major biological as well as psychological differences between men and women. This is especially true not only in HOW men and women communicate differently but also in WHY we communicate. It's probably a good idea to accept these differences as fundamental truths. Like gravity, you can't touch it or smell it or see it but if you've ever fallen on your face, you know it's there.

In order to help you understand what is actually going on, I am going to outline some major communication differences in a way that might help you understand what your woman does or does not want from you and why you seem to be in trouble most of the time.

Ready?

1) MOST WOMEN ENJOY TALKING

It's not actually the talking they enjoy, it's the relating. Women are built for relationships. Let me demonstrate with this example:

If you watch a little girl of say, four years old playing, they might be having a pretend tea party or a pretend birthday party for one of their stuffed animals. Naturally, they would have invited the rest of their stuffed animals to this party. Each stuffed animal would have a name and a personality and there is always some interaction going on. Now, the drama. Snuffy the snake doesn't like Barry the beaver because Barry wasn't nice to Snuffy's friend Gloria the gorilla. So, the little girl will (hopefully) have Snuffy and Barry work it out so they can be friends. Barry will apologize to Gloria and then everyone will be happy again and get back to the pretend party. The little girl will feel good because she helped her stuffed animals work through a potential crisis.

Now let's take a look at a four year old boy at play. In his right hand there is the dreaded T-Rex. In his left hand there is the ever dangerous raptor. They see each other and they prepare for combat. They growl and hiss and then the inevitable happens, they rush at each other with teeth and claws and basic mayhem as they fight to the death.

In other words: girls relate, boys dominate.

So gentlemen, we have been at a disadvantage from the very beginning. So just remember, it's not your fault and it doesn't mean you're a bad person. You're just a man.

So let's get back to difference #1. There you are, minding your own business, wondering if the NFL should expand their season when your woman comes in and starts to talk to you. Now, you may be wondering (if you're listening at all):

> Why is she telling me all this?
> Is there some problem I need to take care of?
> Do I need to do something?
> That's not the way I would have handled it.

Congratulations! You are responding like a true man. You are built for action, for solutions. The time for talking is over; the time for doing is now. You begin, in your manly way, to explain to your woman exactly what she did wrong and how she needs to do it the way you would have done it. You offer suggestions, solutions and sound manly advice. But does she appreciate that? No she doesn't! Instead she gives you that look that you have seen so often and shakes her head mumbling something like, "Why do I bother even trying to talk to you?" and she leaves.

And you, yes you. You sit there and wonder what exactly just happened.

Later, when she explains it to you (again!) you will simply wonder why she gets so upset. Well, I'll explain it to you.

The first thing you should know is, SHE DOESN'T NEED YOUR HELP! She knows exactly what to do in order to resolve whatever she needs to resolve. There is nothing wrong, nothing to fix. She just wants you to listen. If she needs your help figuring something out SHE WILL ASK YOU!

Yes, she has told you this how many times? The fact that she has to keep telling you means that you do not listen to her. And this brings us to the second part in communication with your woman

2) WOMAN WANT YOU TO LISTEN

I realize this is a tough one, so I better explain what listening is. Maybe I should start with what listening is not.

Listening is NOT getting ready to talk. Listening is NOT trying to get your two cents in. Listening is NOT sitting there thinking "When is she ever going to stop." Listening is NOT thinking about how you can ever so slyly take a peak at the Red Sox game to see what the score is. Listening is NOT feeling like you have to defend yourself.

Listening is no more complicated that the word. It simply means you are paying attention.

So let's look at an example where your woman comes home and she is relating her day to you. Listening means being interested in what your woman is telling you. Maybe even asking a question. Believe me when I tell you, your woman listens to every story you tell. She remembers the names of the people you talk about and what it was you were doing with them.

Quick question. Do you remember the names of ANY of the people your woman talks about?

I didn't think so.

5

You don't have to care about your woman's coworkers, you just have to care that your woman wants to tell you about them. You know how, when you want to talk about some work issue, how important it feels to you and how much of your emotional self is tied up in the story? Well, your woman feels the same way when she talks about her work or home life.

3) WOMEN DON'T GET OVER THINGS AS QUICKLY AS MEN

When you're a guy and you're with your guy friends and someone insults you, you insult them back. If the insult is any good, the rest of the guys might join in as an appreciative audience. The insults can go on throughout the night (or until you run out of beer). This is all forgotten the next day and you're all best friends again ready to at it on the next boy's night out.

Women don't do this. If you insult a woman, she actually gets her feelings hurt. The next day she is not all that forgiving and she may be waiting for some kind of acknowledgement on your part that you made a mistake (also known as an apology). Your tendency will be to try to minimize the insult (Oh come on, it wasn't that bad.). Or you may try to deflect it (You know you've said worse things to me.) Or you may want to go on the attack (I think you just take things way too personally.) Or you may go right for the jugular (You're just like your mother).

Any of these responses will land you in the doghouse for days at a time.

If you inadvertently insult your woman (and what man in his right mind would do it on purpose), then you will need to "undo" your error. Without recognition and ownership of the insult, you will cause your woman to think you really don't care. And if your woman believes you don't care then she will end up wondering why she should care. And you know where that leads. Before this can happen you will need to apologize. Try this; "Honey, I'm sorry. I didn't mean to hurt your feelings."

Go ahead, try it. One word at a time. Practice it while you're driving home from work. And try to mean it when you say it. Women know when men are lying and it just insults them even more.

CHAPTER 3

TEN MAJOR DIFFERENCES BETWEEN MEN AND WOMEN

OK, so far, so good. You're still reading (or pretending to) and that's a good sign. There is hope for you yet.

I now want to tell you something that you already know and that's been pounded into you since the printing press was invented.

MEN AND WOMEN ARE DIFFERENT

But we need to put this into terms that you, the lowly man, can truly understand. Let's begin:

DIFFERENCE #1) WOMEN REMEMBER EVERYTHING

Unlike you, oh forgetful one, if you tell a woman something she will remember it for the rest of her life. This means you have to pay attention to the things you tell your woman because if you ever contradict yourself later on, you're screwed. Let me give you an example:

Let's say you and your friend Sam decide to go to a strip club one night after work but you don't want to tell your women (figuring that they might have some opinion about it and not a good one). So, instead of telling your women where you're really going, the two of you come up with a story about how you went to the local March-of-Dimes golf tournament to help those poor unfortunate kids by raising money for research. (You may burn in hell for that.) And let's say your woman not only buys it but you score major man points along the way.

Now, fast forward about fifteen years. You and Sam and your women are at a barbeque having a good time when Sam turns to you and says something like, "You know, we ought to try a golf tournament some day. I hear they're a blast."

The two women look at each other and one of them finally says, "I thought you two did the March-of-dimes tournament."

Now, let's stop the movie right there because you and Sam are nailed. First of all, you have no idea what your woman is talking about because you forgot that story about ten minutes after you congratulated yourself on how clever you were. Second of all, you now know you forgot it but somehow you have to come up with a convincing second lie that will cover the first lie.

"Oh, yea, the March-of-Dimes tournament" you hear yourself saying. And Sam chimes in, "But that was different." "Yea, that was different." You and Sam nod at each other thinking that you could now focus on your cooking but even the ribs are now shaking their heads at you whispering, "You're dog meat big man."

"How was that different?" one of the women might ask.

Yes, my friend, how was that different and what are you going to say now that could possibly get you off the hook?

Next time just save yourself a lot of grief. Tell her the truth. She may not like it but at least you didn't lie to her.

DIFFERENCE #2) WOMEN LIKE TO PROCESS

What does this actually mean?

Let me explain.

"Process" is another word for "talk". And as I've already explained, women love to talk. So, let's say you've just come from a nice party with your neighbors during which time you had a few beverages consisting of fermented fruits and grains. You were having a good old time. You talked about the weather, about baseball, about the stock market, about your dog, your kids…whatever it was, you were there, engaged and present. You thought the party was pretty good (and you got to sneak away with some of the guys and catch the second half of the Celtics and Lakers game).

On the way home your woman starts to tell you about her experience of the night. It seems that Joanne, Bill's woman told her that they were having problems in their marriage and started seeing a couple's counselor, and Mary, Sam's woman, told her Sam might get laid off and they're worried about keeping the house. And also, Sue, Ken's woman told her their son was struggling in school and they might have to take him out and find a new school for him. Then she asks you how the men were feeling about all this.

So, you review the evening in your mind and pick out the relevant pieces of information. You seem to remember the guys talking about work but nothing about their concerns (other then the typical bitchin' about their bosses). Then you remember the Celtics won and there were mixed feelings about that but nothing about anyone's kid. You also remember how that new wife (you forgot the name of the husband) was looking kind of hot and you were enjoying some kind of fantasy about her. There was really nothing else you can think of.

You do, however, remember that the food wasn't as good as it could have been but you decide not to share this with your woman because she may think that's trivial compared to the other things she's thinking about.

Finally, you have to confess that the guys really didn't talk about any of that stuff.

You notice how your woman seems to take that in as another confirmation of the lack of any interpersonal connection that men have with each other.

The final bit of processing occurs when your woman asks you, "What did you think of that new couple?"

OK, now bells and alarms should be going off all over the place in your head. You know instinctively that your woman is really asking you what you thought of the new woman. Armed with the knowledge that women remember everything and that when you're part of a couple there are no such things as "other women" (something you will hear more about in a later chapter), you have a couple of options.

Option #1: "The new couple? Yea, he seemed like a nice guy. I didn't really notice his wife that much, how was she?"

OK, this is not so bad. You covered the right points and gave your woman the impression that you might not actually be having intense sexual fantasies about the new woman.

Or how about this?

Option#2: "You mean, what did I think of the new woman in our little group?" You stop what you're doing, grab your woman passionately and plant a wet one right on her ruby reds. "Sweetie, as long as I have you, there is no other woman in the world that I would even give a second look to."

This is romance novel material. Your woman would probably give you a playful tap on the shoulder and mutter "sure, wise guy" but she will secretly love it.

But since you probably won't be doing option #2 at least you have option #1 to fall back on.

DIFFERENCE #3) WOMEN LIKE TO STAY IN CONTACT WITH THEIR FRIENDS AND FAMILY

This may seem like black magic to you but most women keep their relationships forever. They may still have conversations with other women they've known since birth. While you barely remember the names of the people you work with on a daily basis, your woman knows intimate details of her childhood friend who lives about three thousand miles away.

What this means to you is that, since we know how woman like to communicate, they will be spending time on the phone or on the computer with them. You will not understand this. It will be both mysterious and confusing. You will not understand how your woman (or anyone for that matter) could spend that amount of time maintaining relationships. You fail to see the value in that. (This will become clearer to you after you retire and you follow your woman around from morning to night because you don't know what to do with yourself and you never bothered to maintain any other relationships).

After your woman is done talking to her family or friends she will want to tell you all about it. Here's where the listening part comes in. You may not care. You may not even know these people but you will have to listen. And this brings us to the next major difference between men and women.

DIFFERENCE #4) WOMEN LIKE TO INVOLVE YOU IN THEIR LIVES

Your woman actually wants you to know what is going on for her. She would like you to know a lot of things about her. So before reading, you might want to take this brief little quiz that will let you know just how much you do know about your woman.

1) What are the sizes of any article of clothing your woman wears?

2) What is your woman's favorite author or actor or TV star?

3) How does your woman feel about her boss (or your boss if she doesn't have one)?

4) What is your woman's favorite color? Song? Article of clothing?

5) How does your woman feel about her brothers and

sisters (if she has any)?

6) What are your woman's political views? What gets her angry? What makes her cry?

I will bet you real money that your woman knows every one of these things about you.

Every so often, your woman throws in a pop quiz just to see if you've been paying attention. So there you are, practicing all your listening skills. You maintain eye contact, appear interested and from time to time you pick up a word she says. Her voice has a soothing hum to it so you drift off to thinking about when supper's due…and then her voice stops. Somewhere inside your mind you recognize that the inflection at the end of her last statement was a question. Now you panic! Your woman just asked you a question. You're pretty sure it pertains to whatever it was she was just talking about. You look across the table where she sits waiting for your response. Seconds go by…sweat starts to present itself across your forehead…what do you do now?

Option #1: You look at her sincerely, deeply into her eyes and say, "I don't know honey, that's really a tough question."

She replies, "I asked you if you could pick up our daughter from skating. How is that complicated?"

Or how about:

Option #2: You look across the table and say as honestly as you can, "I'm sorry sweetie; I kind of drifted off for a second and missed the question. What was that again?"

One of the really big lessons I hope you take away from this book is the following:

DON'T LIE TO YOUR WOMAN

Save yourself (and her) a lot of grief and time and energy. She's going to figure it out anyway, so just tell her. And add the apology while you're telling her. It will help her believe you.

DIFFERENCE #5) YOUR WOMAN WILL NEVER LOVE SPORTS THE WAY YOU DO (and I do mean never).

You, oh fearless one, could go on and on about the upcoming season and the draft and the players and averages and injury reports and playoff chances and on and on and on. By now, if you have learned anything about your woman (or perhaps women in general) is that women are typically NOT sports fanatics.

Oh, they may seem politely interested and may actually care who won (especially during the playoffs) but they don't care that much.

Now, your woman has an impression of you as a fairly normal kind of guy (except for those little quirky things you do that no one else knows about). This impression goes out the door whenever she sees you screaming at the television set because of some horrific play or score or call. Then she gets to watch you pace around the house muttering things to yourself such as, "I can't believe it!" or "How could they have chocked so bad?!" Or the ever popular, "Stupid! Stupid! Stupid!"

She suggests that you should probably call some friends over for the next game so you'd have someone to yell at the TV with. But as we all know, men don't do that. We don't do relationships that well and we certainly don't ask for things. So that means out of the 100 million adult men in the country about 99 million of them will be home alone watching their favorite sporting event while yelling at the TV set. (If only we could learn how to harness that energy we could power the world-and it's renewable. And it happens every game. This is why men want to have sons, so that they don't have to sit alone yelling at the TV. It seems so much more normal when other people are there doing it with you. For the guys who have daughters, you'll just have to wait until they marry and then you'll have sons-in-law to help you along.

DIFFERENCE #6) WOMEN CARE HOW THEIR MEN LOOK IN PUBLIC.

Here, we're going into new territory so hang on…your woman wants you to make a good impression to the world. Now, I know how much you absolutely LOVE your Mr. Spock T-shirt with "Live long and prosper" written across the back. The one that's about 30 years old and has been washed so much Mr. Spock has been looking like Captain Kirk for the past decade. And I also know how much you LOVE your old running shoes. You know the ones you wear outside to paint and are now covered with more shades of red stain than the San Francisco Bay Bridge. And we all know how much you adore that old "Reverse the Curse" baseball cap that was handed down from your great great grandfather. But the Sox won it in '04 (and again in '07), so it can probably be retired.

And this, combined with your 20 year old jeans, creates what you consider your perfect weekend attire. Even the dog runs and hides when you come out of the bedroom looking like you just escaped from an old beach movie from the 60's.

Your woman takes one look at this and she starts to vibrate. Every bone in her body wants to throw you into a decontamination chamber and have you sterilized. But she restrains herself by simply stating, "You're going out in public looking like that?" And you consider this a compliment.

What your woman knows is that everyone who sees you will think you're an idiot and she actually cares. What she doesn't know is you have absolutely no idea how others see you and you could care less. They should make a board game out of this. It could go on for hours and be highly entertaining to those who end up listening to your conversation.

DIFFERENCE #7) MOST WOMEN DO NOT FIND THE THREE STOOGES PARTILULARLY FUNNY.

Yes, this is where we can truly draw the line between men and women. It's the Three Stooges challenge.

Take two people and place them in a room with a TV tuned to the channel that's playing the Three Stooges marathon. The one who comes running out screaming in about 30 seconds is the woman.

The Three Stooge's phenomenon can be applied to a number of forms of entertainment that men and women disagree on. For example, there's a really good chance that your woman will NEVER go to see any of the Terminator movies with you, or any movie in which the main character is some sort of futuristic weapon. There's a good chance that your woman's first choice of a movie will not involve any plot that includes a man who has a lot of money and spends his time chasing under clad women. Or any plot line that includes a male character who is pushed past his psychological point of no return by the bad guys and has to go on a killing spree until the end of the movie when he, naturally, gets to the big boss and takes him out after a prolonged battle to the end.

See, this is man stuff. This is what it's all about for us. We can't yell at our boss or the cop who just pulled us over for speeding or our mother-in-law (more on that later) but we can watch a big bruiser of a guy (our alter-egos) go around wasting all the bad guys. We actually like this, which amazes our women to no end.

DIFFERENCE 8) MOST WOMEN WANT THEIR HOMES TO LOOK RELATIVELY NEAT.

What does this mean for you?

It means your woman might actually want to participate in this little event called "cleaning".

Listen, I know what you're thinking. Just what the heck is this "cleaning" thing everyone seems to be talking about? You understand that the children must be taught to keep things neat and clean and that even the dog has rules to follow but you never thought it would come to you having to do something. But there will be more on this in an upcoming chapter. Be sure to look for it, it could impact the rest of your life.

DIFFERENCE 9) WOMEN LIKE THINGS TO MATCH

Let's take the following scenario as an example of this:

It is morning and the both of you are getting ready to go to work. You being the well-to-do, man-about-town that you are walk into the closet, take the shirt that is next in line, take the tie that goes with it, grab your pants, your belt socks and shoes (black or brown). Put it all together and you're ready to go to work.

OK, let's see how that works out for your woman. Now for a woman it depends on whether she having a "fat" day or not. Since you're a man you have absolutely NO IDEA what that means.

First, she has to think about what she has already worn this week. Since a lot of men wear nothing but white shirts and some kind of tie with it (really doesn't matter what color since the shirt is white) or work clothes that look amazingly similar from day to day,

They don't have to worry about whether an outfit was seen this week or not or this decade or not. Doesn't matter, every day is the same. Not so for a woman. Every day is another opportunity to be frustrated by her lack of choices and how there is always something about herself that looks bad. As opposed to men who are always amazed by how good they look (no matter what they actually look like).

Does the blouse go with the skirt and will the pants go with the sweater and does it make me look too fat or too busty? Is it too provocative? Does it send the right message? Can you imagine a man getting dressed and looking at himself in the mirror and wondering, "Does this make my penis look too big?"

And then there are the shoes: what color, what style, how high should the heels be? If a man wears shoes to work they're either black or brown. Period.

No wonder it takes women so long to get dressed. They have so many more variables to work through that every day is almost like a mini therapy session.

Men, if you live to be a thousand years old you still won't really get it. You just have to know it is one of the things that make men and women different.

And finally,

DIFFERENCE 10) WOMEN ARE VERY SELF CRITICAL

You may have heard this before but it is definitely worth repeating. You take the most beautiful woman in the world and put her in front of the mirror and she will find a hundred things wrong with her face. Her ears are too this or her nose is too that or her lips are whatever but it will be a reminder to her of how imperfect she is.

You, being the manly man that you are, will look in the mirror and find all those things that are good about you. Sure, maybe your gut is too big but that's OK because every day you see guys whose guts are even bigger. And sure, maybe your hairline is receding a bit but hey, at least you still have hair, and on and on and on.

You will find someway to feel good about how you look no matter how portly (men are never fat) you are. Women will find the least little bit of loose skin and suddenly they're 50 lbs overweight.

Men have an uncanny ability to look at themselves and no matter how nasty they actually look, find all the things they like about themselves. They will believe that women everywhere will want them. This is our gift and one that we need to teach to our wives because they see every spot, blemish, wrinkle and whatever else it is on their body that reminds them that they are not very attractive.

CHAPTER 4

THE TEN BIGGEST MISTAKES MEN MAKE AFTER THEY ARE IN A RELATIONSHIP

So now you've spent some time getting to know your woman better and possibly even gaining some insight into how she is different from you. Now we'll be focusing on you, and this is as good a place to start as any.

It's hard to believe that you may have actually made some mistakes in your relationship. I know, you're thinking that none of this has anything to do with you and it's all about "her". But I'm afraid I've got some news for you, you are part of this relationship. Yea it sounds pretty dumb but the sooner you realize that you contribute to everything, good and bad, that happens in this relationship, the sooner we can all get around to helping you see what that is.

As a start, I'd like to present to you some basic mistakes men make in their relationships. Oh, and don't feel alone, this happens much more often then you think…just ask the women.

MISTAKE #1) (This is probably the biggest mistake you could ever make in any relationship) MEN STOP SEDUCING THEIR WOMEN

What does this mean, exactly? Well, think back to when you first met and you were a playful little bugger and you couldn't keep your hands off of her. You would pursue her day and night just for the pleasure of being able to be close to her or touch her. You would give her random kisses or hugs. You'd tell her how great she looked. You were curious, interested and flirtatious. Three years later the most effort you put into an evening of sexual intercourse consists of turning the TV off early. And just to show your sacrifice, you'll do it before the game is even over. What a man! Men, due to our limited brain capacity, we get confused and frustrated when our women don't just jump at the chance to have sex with us. Don't they realize what studs we are and that we could have ANY woman we wanted? They should feel lucky…even privileged that they have a guy like us around to allow them to have sex with. And when they say NO to us, we end up feeling like little rejected puppy dogs.

"How could they do this to us?" we wonder. After all we do for them. And then we start to pout, as if our favorite toy was just taken away from us. We might even get defensive and angry (boy this will get you a lot of sex).

Meanwhile, your woman is wondering just where did that man go who use to charm her and cozy up to her and give her all that time and attention. She keeps looking for him but in return all she gets is a shadow of that man.

You want a happy relationship? Then remember this and remember it always, a relationship is a living thing. You must feed it and nurture it or it will die. You have to also know that your woman cannot provide sex on demand. (More about this in a later chapter.)

MISTAKE #2) MEN BELIEVE THEIR WOMEN ARE RESPONSIBLE FOR THEIR MEMORY

Does this sound familiar, "Honey, have you seen my black tie?" or socks or keys? How about, "What time do we have to be at the Johnson's party?" or, "Who's going to be there?" Men fully expect that their woman will remember everything they need to know for them. And because of this we make a conscious decision not to know how to do things. We lose track of time, where we put things and basically how to think. I mean, why bother? We have our woman right there to do all our thinking for us. Years later, after we retire, we will follow our wives around asking things like, "Honey, what do I do with my life now?"

What we end up doing is making our woman responsible for our behavior. This begins a nasty pattern in which we continue to find more and more things for our woman to be responsible for until such time as our woman decides she will no longer be responsible for anything. Then we are screwed. How about this for a start; buy a watch, write things down, look at the calendar that's hanging in the kitchen, listen to what your woman tells you and remember it.

MISTAKE #3) MEN BELIEVE THEY ARE IN A RE-LATIONSHIP WITH THEIR MOTHER.

What does this mean exactly? This means that men think they should be taken care of (just like good old mom use to do) and be able to do whatever it is they want. This means having a set of expectations that might include having a woman who will cook for them or do laundry for them or the cleaning or being sympathetic when you come home after a long hard day's worth of work. This means the man has to think only of his needs (because, as we all know, moms have no needs when it comes to their children).

It often comes as a surprise to a man that his woman has needs too. Unfortunately, her needs are NOT on his radar. Her needs are mysterious and unknowable. Her needs can really never be met. (So why even try...?) Her needs are too much and too soon and too often. His mother never had any needs so why should his woman?

What you might have to do in this case is actually try to picture your mother as a woman and think about how things must have been for her. You may have to challenge that old thinking a bit and replace it with some new and improved thinking.

MISTAKE #4) MEN TURN THEIR WOMEN INTO NAGS

Somewhere in the middle of the relationship the man wakes up to find that his woman is not very happy with him. She seems to always be complaining about something, nagging him about doing this or doing that. At this point the man gets angry and defensive and says things about how hard he works and about how he is never appreciated for what he does and can't for one minute everyone just leave him alone so he can relax!

This is not good for many reasons. The first is you, the man, feel justified in what you are saying. In your world, you come home and the first thing you realize is your woman is telling you to do something. And doesn't it seem to you as if she is always telling you to do something? So all you are aware of is her nagging.

So, sit down because I have something important to tell you. Ready? Hold on, because here it comes…you created this person who you see in front of you giving you so much trouble. I know it's hard to believe but it is true none the less. This woman who is angry and frustrated and who has become something she doesn't want to be is this way because of you. "How did this happen?" you might ask. Let me explain;

You do not listen when your woman is talking to you.

It is no harder to figure out than that. Remember in the beginning of the relationship how you listened to every word she said? And how somewhere along the line you decided that listening wasn't very important any longer and you stopped? Who knows why? Maybe because it was too hard for you to keep paying attention or maybe you really didn't care to begin with but now you don't even pretend.

So, since you didn't hear what your woman said, she now goes back to you to ask why you didn't do that thing she thought you were going to do. Since you don't even remember what she asked, you can either admit that you weren't paying attention or simply get defensive and go back to what you were doing. So now she has to ask you again to do whatever it was that you said you would do but didn't. And now, since she has little faith that you will actually do this thing, she has to check up on you. So she will ask, "Did you do that thing I asked you to do?" Since you didn't do it, you will now get defensive and angry. Now she either has to escalate and get louder (perhaps even calling you names) or she gives up and does it herself. When she does it herself she, at least, leaves you alone. But not so quick. This will go down in her book as a failure on your part to do whatever it was you were suppose to do. And she will remember (remember?). She might even stop asking you to do things.

Now you might actually think this is good, but it's not. It will be the first in a long line of disappointments. Each disappointment that does not get resolved (as in you saying you're sorry and next time doing the thing she wants done), leads to a gap…and each gap will collect and end up becoming a crevice. And then the crevice becomes a canyon and then the canyon grows until it is the Grand Canyon. This is known as the erosion of intimacy (more on this in another chapter).

I do hate to use words like intimacy with men because it confuses them so. So, just remember, relationships don't fall apart in huge chunks but rather little bit by little bit. When it's small you still have a chance to fix it, but if you let these things go too long they will destroy your relationship. This is not just with your women but with all women.

So the next time you realize you didn't do something you told your wife you were doing to do, apologize, get off your butt and do it…you'll be happy you did.

MISTAKE #5) MEN LIE TO THEIR WOMEN

If you've been paying attention you have seen this before and you will probably see it again. DO NOT LIE TO YOUR WOMAN. Here are a few good reasons why,

1) They don't like it

2) They will find out the truth eventually

3) They know when you are lying.

For a lie to succeed (at least temporarily) you must convince your woman that you are definitely telling the truth. This will force her to choose between you and her inner voice that is telling her that you are full of it. If she chooses you over her own inner voice, she is doing that based totally on faith that you would never lie to her. This trust that she has in you is worth its weight in gold and can never be replaced after it's broken. Please remember this before you tell her the lie. As mentioned before, even if you know that she'll be angry at you, at least you told her and she knows that and you will win huge man points for that.

If you lie she will eventually find out and then she will question everything you have done since the day she met you. And you will hate this.

So a good rule of thumb is, DON'T LIE!

MISTAKE #6) MEN BELIEVE THEIR MONEY IS THEIR MONEY

Ah yes, the money. People will tell me their deepest darkest secrets but when it comes to their money, they don't want anyone to know. If we can think of money as the number one drug in America (or the world?) then we can better understand why no one wants you to know too much about how much they got or where they keep it. That being said, one of the jobs of any two people in their relationship is knowing how to discuss (or even share money.)

Whether you're dating or are married with kids, the subject of money WILL come up and you will have to decide just how important your money is to you. One of the biggest mistakes a man can make is thinking that the money he makes is all his.

Well, actually is you're just dating, it is, in fact, all his. But when things heat up and there is much more sharing than men have to find a way to share their money as well. Women tend to sit back and observe. Even when you don't think you're teaching her anything about yourself, your woman learns about who you are just by observing how you operate in the world. This includes how you spend your money and how generous you are (or are not).

So, if you buy yourself a lot of toys but balk whenever your woman wants to buy a new dress or shoes, then you're not really getting the message.

MISTAKE 7) MEN SIDE WITH THEIR FAMILY/MOTHER OVER THEIR WOMAN.

This one gets bigger as the relationship becomes more serious but any man who listens to his mother over his wife is asking for a very short relationship. Likewise, if you allow your family to influence you too much over the woman you've been dating then don't expect to be dating for very long.

A woman wants an independent man, not someone who is checking in with his family to see what he should do.

And by the way men, if you really want to end a relationship, just tell your woman how much better your mother does things.

MISTAKE #8) MEN FLIRT WITH OTHER WOMEN (EVEN WHEN THEY'RE WITH THEIR WOMAN)

Men, if you want to have a happy relationship and if you really don't want to screw this one up, then you have to remember one thing very clearly (and I'll be mentioning it again). WHEN YOU'RE IN A RELATIONSHIP WITH SOMEONE THERE ARE NO OTHER WOMEN.

MISTAKE #9) MEN BELIEVE THEIR WOMEN SHOULD BE READY FOR SEX ALL THE TIME

I'm not sure I need to go into much detail here except for the fact that a man's sex drive is typically greater than a woman's. There is probably nothing else in the world that is known as well as this is known. As the saying goes, "Women need a reason to have sex; men just need a place."

Do I really have to go into all the details about how women are really after intimacy as opposed to sex? While women can enjoy sex as much as men, it's really the other things that go along with it that make it valuable for them. Haven't you heard this enough by now? Do you really need me to say it again? I didn't think so.

MISTAKE #10) MEN MAKE OTHER THINGS MORE IMPORTANT THEN THEIR RELATIONSHIPS

This is one of those signs that I look for that tells me whether I'm sitting with a couple who will make it or not. If a man has anything more important in his life than his relationship (assuming we're talking about a long- term relationship or a marriage) then his woman will know that (men aren't very good at hiding their true feelings). For a relationship to work it must be the highest priority for a man. Anything less and you have a relationship that's not going to be very happy for very long.

CHAPTER 5

BECOMING A COUPLE

I'm not exactly sure when two people become a couple and I'm sure it varies from couple to couple but when you ask the question, "When did you know you were a couple?" you get different answers. For you, the American Man that you are (regardless of what country you came from), the question, "Am I in a relationship?" might occasionally come up for you.

Usually this question does not occur to you until the woman you've been dating for the past…I don't know….10 years, turns to you one fateful night and says, "Just where are we going with our relationship?"

Up until that moment, you didn't even know you were in a relationship. I believe that try as they might, men need some help in determining if they are in an official "relationship" or not.

Let's start with Jill and Ken, a couple I've been working with for a while:

Therapist: So, when did you know you guys were a couple?

Jill: When he started calling me every day and wanting to know how I was doing.

Ken: What do you mean a couple?

Jill: Or it could have been when he started sending me flowers after we spent a romantic weekend together.

Ken: You know the word "couple" could mean a lot of different things

Jill: Maybe when he cried the night I told him he hurt my feelings.

Ken: It's not that we're, you know, together all the time. I still see my friends from time to time.

Maybe this chapter should be called "How to pretend you're really not in a relationship when you've been in one for the past two years". Because from the sound of this couple and many others, the man is usually the last one to know.

Here are some ways men pretend they're not in a relationship:

1) We're not living together.

2) We're not engaged.

3) We have separate checking accounts.

4) I don't keep any of my clothes over her place.

5) I haven't met her parents.

6) We still have our own apartments.

7) I don't talk to her every day.

8) I still go out with the guys.

9) I'm still attracted to other women. (more on this one later)

And on and on...

So, in the spirit of helping you out, let me tell you the signs that you are actually in a relationship:

1) Face it guys, if you're reading this book, you're in a relationship.

2) You're married. (that's a big clue!)

3) You're standing in front of a large group of people in a church, temple, large hall, backyard, etc. You are in a tux and the woman you've been dating or living with for the past year or two is walking toward you dressed entirely in white.

4) You find yourself going to a "chick flick" because it was her turn to pick a movie.

5) You realize you know where she is all day, every day.

6) You realize that all of her friends know you and all of your friends know her.

7) You find yourself thinking about how she might feel if you did a particular thing (which also means you should probably not be doing the particular thing you've been thinking about doing).

8) You have an extra toothbrush that lives in her apartment (and she has one at yours).

9) You haven't slept in your bed for about two weeks now (or she hasn't slept in hers).

10) Your dog likes her more then he likes you.

11) You call her in the middle of the day just so you can hear her voice (and you have no idea why and wouldn't admit to it under threat of torture).

12) Your Saturday night dates have expanded to Saturday night, Sunday morning, afternoon and evening.

13) You read the Sunday paper together with coffee and the only thing breaking through the jazz music playing in the background is an occasional comment about something newsworthy.

14) You know her favorite color and her favorite flowers.

15) She uses the "L" word (and so do you).

16) You know how she takes her coffee (or tea).

17) When you go home to visit your family everyone asks you, "So, how is….(fill in her name, pal).

18) You slept over her place and left some clothes there. The next time you're there they've been washed and folded and now occupy a special place in one of her drawers.

19) You have the same address.

20) You start making holiday plans, about six months in advance.

21) You vacation together.

22) You attend her cousins wedding with her and every relative you are introduced to has that "you're next" look in their eyes.

23) Slowly but surely, all the people you hang out with are coupled.

24) You taste each other's food when you go out to eat (or she lets you finish her meal).

25) She buys you clothes (and knows your size).

And I'm sure there are so many other little signs that will suggest to you you're in a relationship, but the point is,

CONGRATULATIONS! YOU ARE A COUPLE!

What does this mean exactly? It means you are now sharing your time, space and stuff with another person. It also means you are now sharing getting your needs met.

See, when you were single, the only needs you had to think about were yours and yours alone. When you're part of a couple, your needs are only half the equation, not the full equation.

So, you may be wondering, how do I make sure I'll get my needs met? If you're wondering that (and that alone) then you may not actually be ready for a relationship. What you should be wondering is, "Will I be able to meet the needs of my woman?" as well as, "Will we learn how to meet each other's needs?"

With this is mind, I'd like to bring you to the next stage which follows immediately after becoming a couple and which may explain a bit better why you're having so much trouble with this "meeting her needs" stuff.

CHAPTER 6

WHAT IT MEANS TO BE A COUPLE

If you made it this far (in your life, not the book), then you are officially a couple. Of course, you may already know this (especially if you're married or living together). What you may not know is exactly what that means. This chapter is designed to let you know what you signed on for (whether you know it or not).

Now, you might feel proud of yourself that you went ahead and became part of a committed relationship, that you went and showed the world that you were mature enough to take the "plunge". And you may also be naïve enough to think that that was all you had to do. So you sit in your chair in the living room having a beer and watching the game and thinking to yourself, "You know this isn't so bad."

Ah, my friend, if you only knew.

Getting into a relationship is one thing. STAYING in a relationship is something quite different.

EMOTIONAL CONTRACTING

The difference between whether you can maintain a long-term relationship or not is whether you comply with the "emotional contract" you made.

"Emotional contract"? You ask innocently.

"Yes", I answer. And because you have no idea what that actually means, I will have to explain it to you.

All relationships are based on the emotional contract that two people write out together. As the name implies, this is a contract regarding the feelings and needs of the two people who are in the relationship. This contract is written and rewritten over the life of the relationship as to insure that the needs of the two people in the relationship will be addressed and met.

But you seem a bit confused. Actually you seem a lot confused. You see, this type of contract differs from other contracts because 1) it is unconscious and 2) it is unwritten. In fact, very often the first time you may realize you have signed an emotional contract is when you have broken it.

So what actually is an "emotional contract"? Well, let's first look at the words. To break it down into its basic parts, "emotional contract" has two words pieced together: "Emotional" and "contract."

Let's start with contract. (The easier of the two).

A contract is, by definition, an agreement between two people regarding the specific thing they are contracting over. That's pretty straightforward. A good contract is clear and specific in the nature of the goods or service being contracted for.

Emotions are going to be a bit harder. They are your feelings.

Let's look at it this way: you're watching your favorite baseball team play an important division rival. You are watching the game under an implied contract. The contract is simply that the team will do its best to win as many games as they possibly can. To that end, the individuals on that team will play the best baseball they know how to play. If the team plays hard and each player gives their best, but they still lose, you might be sad about that but you're not going to be that angry. On the other hand, if you believe the players did not play their best and they lost because of that, you will become extremely angry.

Why?

Because they broke the contract. They didn't play their best. Now you feel cheated, duped, wronged…everything that your woman feels about you if she feels you didn't live up to the contract you agreed to.

Is this getting clearer?

The other way to think about emotional contracting is to think about a seed you just planted into a cup of soil. While you may not be able to see anything, that seed is laying down a root system and collecting valuable nutrients. You won't see any result from that until some manner of time goes by. Even though you can't see it, it doesn't mean that nothing is going on.

That's how you need to think about an emotional contract. Even though you may not be aware of it, there's a lot of work going on underneath the surface.

So what exactly IS going on beneath the surface? Are you sure you want to know?

From the very start of getting to know someone you are negotiating your emotional contract. You both have needs that you're trying to get met. Some of those needs you may not even be aware of but that doesn't stop the process. In fact, why don't you stop right now and think to yourself, "What exactly do I need from this relationship?"

Time's up! How did you do? I bet you didn't even take the time to think about it, did you? No wonder your woman is so angry at you.

When it comes to an emotional contract the better you know yourself and your feelings, the better you'll be at contracting with your woman. If you have little idea of how you feel or how you express your feelings, then you're going to end up in a situation in which you have no idea what's going on or how you got there.

Let's take "teasing" as an example.

So let's say you like to tease your woman sometimes and let's say you think it's really cute. The scenario might go something like this: You're at a party and you're with a bunch of friends. Everyone's having a good time. The conversation turns to how your woman tried to fix something in the kitchen and you make some kind of comment like, "Yeah, your fixing things is about as good as your cooking."

Now you think this is a riot. You're laughing, thinking, "good one!" However, when you take a second and glance over to where your woman is standing she's not laughing. In fact, she's staring…no, not staring, glaring…no, not normal glaring. It's more like if she could bore a hole to the center of your brain with her super x-ray vision, she'd be doing it right now.

Now, she won't say anything to you there and then because she doesn't want to get into it with all your friends there. No, she'll wait until you're driving home from the party and then you'll hear about it.

"So, what was that crack you made about my cooking?"

Your first move will be to get defensive.

"Oh, come on…I was just joking around."

Just joking around. So how many times have you insulted your woman in public under the pretense that you were just "joking around"? I bet she remembers because every time you do it she is humiliated.

I can hear you now…"Oh come on, man. That's a bit extreme, don't you think?"

Yeah, it's always about how someone is misinterpreting you. It's never about what YOU'RE doing.

Many a truth has been disguised as a joke and the butt of the joke is never you, is it? If you don't like how your woman cooks then either you'll have to find a more effective way to tell her or you need to learn to cook. But you don't wait until you're at a party and let it all hang out under the pretense of a joke. The problem is you weren't even aware that you felt that way. It just sort of came out and now you've got to deal with it.

By doing what you did, you broke the contract. You hurt her feelings. I realize that the last thing a man wants to face is that he hurt someone's feelings, because that means you're going to have to take responsibility for what you did. And even worse, it means you won't be able to use humor as a weapon anymore because it's clear what you're doing. However, you may be the last one to know that.

Hurting people through your version of humor is still hurting people and it's still breaking the contract.

Here's another nice example for you. Your girlfriend tells you her father and mother are coming in for the weekend and she would like you to join them for dinner Saturday night. You say you will and that seems to be the end of it. However, for some strange reason you find it a perfectly good idea to party all night long on Friday night and you don't get home until about 6:00 on Saturday morning. You are hung over, spaced out and look like someone just dragged you through a mud pit. You also have no idea of what time it is or what's going on that evening. You end up hitting the sack and sleep the entire day away. It's about 6:00 PM when you finally crawl out of bed to notice there are several missed messages on your phone. They're from your girlfriend.

Suddenly the little gray matter that you often refer to as your "brain" starts releasing chemicals through your neuro-muscular system. You remember that you were due to be at your girlfriend's place by 5:00 so you could chat with her and her parents until it was time to go to dinner. You call her. I imagine you could probably script out the conversation that will go on when she finds out that not only will you not be able to be at her place (an hour ago) but you won't be making it for dinner either. So now, this woman who you've been dating for awhile (long enough so that she wanted you to meet her parents) has to go back to her parents and make up some excuse why you weren't there.

Congratulations! You have just managed to end another in a series of relationships and you have no idea what happened. You accepted responsibility for the screw up and apologized. You figure she might be mad at you for awhile but then she would get over it.

WRONG!

There is screwing up and then there is SCREWING UP. And this my friend is SCREWING UP.

Do you know what happened? No? I'll tell you.

The adolescent in you beat out the man in you for first place in the "let me show her parents exactly what I think about their daughter" competition.

You think you just ended up letting the night get the better of you. Sorry, Charlie, it was much more than that. Your message to your girlfriend was basically, "Screw you and your parents. I'm going to do whatever I want to."

By deciding to go out and party so hard the night before the meeting, you basically sabotaged the relationship. And you don't even know why. My guess would be that you were so intimidated by the prospect of meeting her parents; you made sure it wasn't going to happen.

There are two ways you can give a message to someone; through your words or through your behavior. Instead of telling your girlfriend how you felt and that you didn't think you were ready to meet her parents (or just didn't want to), you let your behavior do your talking for you.

You broke the contract about communicating your feelings (and yes, you do have them and yes, as noted, they do affect your behavior).

Since everything you do in your relationship is part of the contracting process, you have to watch what you do.

This is another plug for knowing yourself. The less you know about yourself the less you can effectively contract. In the previous scenario, you had no conscious idea of how scared you were to meet the parents in question so your unconscious took over and you communicated that through your actions. Now, if the woman in question were to break off the relationship then you would probably think she over-reacted or you would find some other way to explain it to yourself so that you wouldn't have to face your own feelings.

The healthier you are, the healthier your relationship can be.

CHAPTER 7

THE ADOLESCENT MAN

Up to this point, we've been looking at how you've come to relate (or not) to your woman. We've also tried to look at some of the things that sometimes get in the way of you being a full participant in your relationship. So, I believe we are now ready to take a step closer to you, the Average American Man.

For those of you who are not use to self exploration, and being an Average American Man you probably wouldn't be, here is a word of warning, you may learn things about yourself that you don't want to learn. You may also come to realize what it is that your woman has been talking about when she refers to you in less, than manly, ways.

So, take a deep breath, relax and here we go:

As the chapter title indicates, there are (at least) two basic components to a man's brain, the adolescent and the man.

As mentioned before, women often fall in love with the adolescent (or the little boy in you) and then go looking for the man. If a woman also finds the man then she is fine and may end up falling in love with you (we'll deal with that in another chapter). If she doesn't find the man, she will end up feeling betrayed and used. That should end the relationship. (We'll discuss this more in the next chapter).

So let's look a bit closer at these parts of the man's brain so we can get to know them a bit better.

THE ADOLESCENT

As the name implies, the adolescent in each man is exactly that. It is the 15- year-old who still lives inside of you making 15-year-old decisions and thinking 15-year-old thoughts.

So what do we know about 15-year-olds?

The typical 15-year-old boy is primarily self-absorbed, competitive, needs to win (or be right), is obsessed with girls (or at least their body parts), needs to impress, needs to feel special, is involved with sports (as a spectator or a player), is obsessed with video games, needs to dominate, likes to have fun, is insecure about girls, is focused on the present...I think you get the picture.

The adolescent lives in the mind of every man. Some are more present than others and some are more repressed. Some men see and accept that part of them and let the adolescent out occasionally when it won't cause any irreparable damage. Other men are ruled by the emotions stored in their adolescent and they act accordingly. This is really not good for anyone and can ruin a decent relationship (much to the regret of the woman who wants her man to act like a man). And this brings us to:

THE MAN

Again, as the name implies, this is the part of you that has evolved over time. It is the adult in you (hopefully) starting to take charge. It is the rational working with the emotional to offer a balanced individual.

So what do we think about when we think about what a man is?

A man understands and accepts that the world does not revolve around him. A man understands that he does not own the truth. His opinion is just an opinion, like many of the opinions around him. He understands and accepts his limitations, he realizes that his needs may not always come first and he realizes that sometimes he may have to delay getting what he wants so that someone can get their needs met. A man is willing to accept responsibility for his actions. He strives for intimacy. He is willing to sacrifice. He supports and encourages. He values what others do for him.

A man is not perfect. He does make mistakes or forgets or becomes impatient at times. The difference is, he recognizes it and takes responsibility for it while trying to understand what he did and how he can change.

Now, the man mentioned here is more of an ideal then an actuality. It is something we strive for but few attain (I'm certainly not there-yet). But it's the striving for the ideal that makes the difference. It's the wanting to be a better man that counts. As the expression goes, "I want to be the person that my dog thinks I am".

Since the differences in the Adolescent mind and the Man's mind are so extreme you may wonder just how these two versions of the same person can live in the same brain. Well, clearly, it's not easy.

As an example of how this works, let's take a look at the man at work and the man at home.

The man we are discussing ends up separating himself into two very different versions. In one version he is the professional, high achieving and high functioning worker. He follows the rules, works well with authority (unless there are family issues we don't know about) and is typically well regarded.

This person, we say, is a "mensch".

But take that highly competent man, bring him home, and he turns into...

MUSH BRAIN MAN

At home, he drops things, loses things and forgets how to do things. He can easily end up feeling entitled because he went to work (as if he was the only person in the world who went to work that day). While at work he may supervise or manage other workers and he may be good at it. At home he forgets how to communicate or even speak clearly.

Where did all those skills go? Where did his ability to be clear and focused go? What happened to the "Captain of Industry"?

I'm afraid to say that was all left at work.

You see, somewhere between the door of his office building or truck or bus and the front door of his house, his brain started leaking and by the time he entered his home, his brain had leaked all over the car or roadway and there is very little left.

This is very confusing to woman (mostly because their brains aren't allowed to leak…ever). Let's look at this typical interaction that happens in millions of homes all across the country:

"Honey, could you take out the garbage?"

"The Garbage?"

"Yeah, you know that stuff that smells so bad that we keep it in the garbage can outside the house."

"You need me to do that now?"

"Now would be good."

"Come on…I just got home…I've been working all day and…"

Hold it right there!

You have just pushed it into the "I'm more important than you." category. In this category you will try to prove to your woman that your time and your need to relax are much greater then hers. You have now forced her to remind you that she also works, hard and long. And if your woman is home with kids all day she will now be forced to tell you what it's like chasing your kids around all day.

So what you've managed to do by your response is to minimize and devalue what your woman does all day and look like a jerk in the process.

Do yourself a favor:

TAKE OUT THE FREAKIN' GARBAGE!

Before we leave this particular chapter, you should know that every man has to resolve the conflict between his inner adolescent and his inner man. To do that, it means those two sides of him will have to sit down with each other and work out their differences. There will need to be some sort of compromise that allows the adolescent to still have some fun but not at the expense of the people around him.

Believe it or not, your woman doesn't mind if you need to be an adolescent occasionally as long as it's done with the understanding that you will have to return to being a man before too much time has gone by. She understands that you have to have your hockey game or golf game or movie night or softball game or any of the millions of other things you want to do. That's not the problem. The problem is when the adolescent in you takes charge and overrides the man in you and you start believing and acting as if you are entitled to do whatever you want to do whenever you want to do it.

It's OK to be a kid at times as long as you remember you're actually a man.

CHAPTER 8

THE DELICATE BALANCE OF INTER-DEPENDENT LIVING

Don't you love that title? Don't you wish you knew what it meant? You are now in that very interesting period of time known as the transition from single life to coupled life. It means you are either moving in together or just got married. Either way, it is during this time when we will find out just how willing and capable you are to share your life space as well as the power and control over such space.

Your life is about to look very different. So let's take a look at some of the transition points you will want to pay close attention to.

Before we get started I want to introduce you to three new words that will become part of your everyday vocabulary, (definitions courtesy of dictionary.com)

COMPROMISE: A settlement of differences by mutual concessions.

Oh, this can not be good. It's the word "concessions" that's the bother. Concession, the act of yielding. "Yielding" is not a manly word. It's something that other people do if they're forced to do it. What man is going to voluntarily yield? This is going to be harder than you thought.

In ordinary terms, what this means is, to get something you have to give something and nobody gets everything they want…nobody.

This means finding a middle ground that you both can live with. And, if you're not use to doing that then this will take some practice

NEGOTIATION: Mutual discussion and arrangement of the terms of a transaction or agreement. OK, what could THIS possibly mean? Let's begin with this word "mutual". Mutual. Experienced by each of two (or more) with respect to the other. RESPECT? Not another vocabulary word! Respect. To show consideration for (another person). Consideration? Careful thought. OK, let's see if we have this right. When you discuss issues with your woman, you have to consider her point of view. Are you sure you can do this? I mean it's pretty easy to only think about the thing you want but when you have to think about someone else's needs too? Is your head starting to hurt?

SHARING:

This is our final vocabulary word. Since we have all been through kindergarten we all have some sense of what sharing means but let's make sure we have it right. Sharing. To divide or distribute proportionately. What's proportionately? As in balanced? As in equal? Now, who gets to decide that? I guess that's where negotiation comes in.

All right, if you're still ready to become a couple then we can move on. Armed with some definitions let's see what it means to transition from single life to coupled life.

As previously mentioned, when you are single you can do just about anything you want anytime you want because there is no one there to tell you you can't. If you're a guy living with a bunch of guys then it's not much more removed than living single.

BEING SINGLE

What does being single mean?

Being single means you can eat on any surface you want and you only have to clean up when you feel like cleaning up.

It means you can throw your shoes or your dirty laundry any place you'd like.

You don't have to make your bed. (Is there a man in the world who ever made a bed before he got into a relationship?)

You don't have to do the dishes. Actually you probably don't even have dishes since paper plates are so simple to use and to discard of.

If you go out, you can come home any time you want. And if you've had too much to drink there's no one there waiting to remind you you've had too much to drink.

You can get up from the couch during the middle of a TV show without anyone asking, "Where are you going?" or, "While you're up could you get me some water?"

You can have frozen foods or eat potato chips and ice cream seven days a week without anyone asking why your diet is so poor.

You can create an exact replica of the Statue of Liberty out of old beer cans and keep it in the middle of your living room.

You can hang every poster of every naked woman ever created anywhere.

You never have to clean your bathroom (you do risk being condemned by the board of health, however).

You can have guys over any time of day or night to watch as many sporting events as you'd like.

You can spend entire weekends trying to master the latest video game that just came out.

You can buy whatever you want without someone asking, "What did you get that for?"

You can wear whatever you want without someone looking at you and asking, "Are you sure you want to be seen in public looking like that?"

You can fall asleep in front of the TV without someone asking, "Are you coming to bed?" (And it's not for sex).

You never have to explain what you are doing to anyone.

You don't have to worry about someone hogging the blankets (although it would probably be you doing the hogging).

You can walk around naked (or in your fabulous boxers).

You can spend all day in the bathroom (although I don't want to know what you're doing there). And you don't need to buy air freshener.

Your bicycle or guitar or golf clubs or whatever it is that's important to you occupies a central position in the middle of whatever room you choose to put it in.

Basically, the only needs you have to consider are yours.

In fact you can do anything you want when you're single except for one very important thing...you can't be in a relationship.

HOW IT STARTS

It begins when you start dating someone, you're starting to hit it off and you're thinking about inviting her over. And then you look at your apartment. I mean, you really look at it. Do you really want her to see how you live? This calls for some serious thought. Let's see...you could borrow someone else's apartment...no, that won't work. You could create a collection of excuses as to why it's not possible for her to come over until, say, the next decade. I don't think she'll buy that.

Well, there's only one other thing you can do...you can clean.

CLEANING

Clean: To make something free from dirt or pollution or matter of any sort that is deemed to be "dirty". (Another vocabulary word.)

I wanted to devote a section of this chapter to something you may know little about but will have to learn a lot more about after you are part of a couple. You will have to learn how to clean. I don't mean the kind of cleaning you're doing now as a single man. I don't think that qualifies as cleaning. No, you're going to have to learn how to clean according to the standards of your woman. And you will learn about many new and interesting things. There are brooms and mops and cleaning products and sponges and all sorts of things that are designed to do one thing and one thing only, keep stuff clean.

Before your woman comes over for the first time you may need a female friend to come over and tell you what you need to do. If your friend stops at your front door, covers her mouth and runs away to throw up in the bushes then you may want to hire a cleaning service (at least until you get the hang of it).

The real test of the future possibility of a relationship is the first time your woman comes over to your place. There you will be, so proud that you spent a good hour (maybe two) getting the place ready for her. Now, you have to watch her facial expressions as she looks around. Does she seem angry? Judgmental? Critical? If she does, she may not be the woman for you. But if she looks around and then looks back at you with the kind of look that people have when they spot a lost puppy and she shakes her head and says, "You really tried didn't you?" And you find yourself looking back at her in a sheepish way while nodding and saying "Yes", then you may have a keeper.

So now that you have an idea of what you're in for, let's quickly move onto the next chapter, which I hope you will find very informative

CHAPTER 9

LIVING WITH A WOMAN

Well, my friend. Here you are. Married or not, you are now sharing physical space. So the question is, have you ever lived with a woman before? No? I mean other than your mother or sisters. Having sisters is good because it can give you some sense of what you're in for. But it's still not quite the same.

So I'm going to give you a sense of what will be happening to you or may have already happened to you that will be challenging you beyond what you're use to.

Let's just go through several things that will become different for you from the moment you two set up your household

EVERYTHING HAS ITS PLACE

This is also known as "the floor is not a place".

Whatever it is, it belongs somewhere. Whether it's a dish, shoes, the computer…there's a place for it and that's where it's supposed to go. If you put something where it's not supposed to be, your woman will tell you, "It doesn't go there."

You may wonder, "How do they know these things?"

I'm not quite sure but I think when they're younger, women go to girl school. And in girl school they teach them all sorts of things about what it means to be a girl. One of the classes is on where to put things. Most of the other classes must be about how to put up with boys, but that's just a guess.

THE KITCHEN

Nowhere is the "everything has its place" rule more evident than in the kitchen. Here you will discover that different types of food get stored in particular ways. You will also discover that there are two basic groups of people in the world: Those who refrigerate ketchup and those who don't.

There are things in kitchens that only women know what to do with and all these things are stored together in one particular drawer in the kitchen. This brings me to the "kitchen drawer" part of the chapter. How is it that women know what drawer to put everything in? How is it that a woman can go to any other woman's house and know where everything in the kitchen is?

And why, is it that in every kitchen in the western world, there always one drawer, usually called "the junk drawer" where everything goes that has no place else to go. It's like the drawer of homeless kitchen stuff. Here's where you'll find the take-out menus, paper clips, calculator, coupons, local phone book, etc. etc. How do women do that?

By the way, it never ceases to amaze me how I could be at Crate and Barrel with my wife and we'll go through the section where they have all these little cooking things and I'll come across something that looks like a cross between a can opener and a grasshopper and I will have no idea what it's for. She takes a look at it and tells me that, yes this is for coring butternut squash when you just need the middle for soup, or some such thing.

You know, I usually feel pretty smart until I come home and have to find something in the kitchen. Even my daughters know where things are and they have since they've been born. My son, however, only goes into the kitchen to eat. He tells me it's scary in there and he's afraid something will jump out of one of the drawers and hurt him.

THE BATHROOM

OK, here is one place that a man will really have to get used to once he starts living with a woman. The typical man's bathroom might include a razor, shaving gel, aftershave lotion, underarm deodorant and a hairbrush or comb. That's it. It can all fit in a small space somewhere in the medicine cabinet. A man typically showers, shaves, puts on deodorant, brushes his teeth and he is on his way. So guys, I want to take some time with you and briefly go over what you are going to find in the bathroom once you are living together.

There's no quiz so you really won't have to remember anything and I doubt if your woman will ever send you out to get any of these products (too many things could go wrong) but you should know what you're getting into. By the way, you will probably have little idea of what a lot of this is for and it's probably better that way.

COSMETICS

You will find that women have a variety of items that they apply on a daily basis. It also appears that they break it down into products for the face, eyes and lips. For the face, women start with what they call "foundation" This is applied with a little round sponge (which you will find in different area of the bathroom sink over time). Next is a "concealer" that is applied with a little brush and then finally "blush" is applied (another brush).

Now we move to the eyes. There is "eyeliner", a pencil. Then there is "eye shadow", which I think is another pencil. Finally we have "mascara" which is another brush that puts stuff on eyelashes.

For the lips we start with "lip liner" (is that another little brush?), then lip color (that's lipstick), and then finally "lip gloss", which is another brush.

So, in other words, when you enter the bathroom there will be at least three jars of something, each with its own sponge or brush. Then there will be three or four smaller containers that each have their own little pencil or brush and then you'll see the lipstick and two other brushes.

None of this includes the mirrors and bright lights that seem to be part of the process. By the way, all this will require a room of its own, so make sure there is plenty of space in the bathroom area or you'll be brushing your teeth with one of the "eyeliner" brushes.

As an aside, you may also want to keep your eyes open for nail polish and nail polish remover. They can appear almost anywhere and it's never safe to use them in an enclosed space.

LAUNDRY

This is another interesting area for men who always thought they knew what they were doing, but it turns out they didn't. And I believe manufacturers of laundry equipment make their machines knowing full well that only women can work them. For example, if you look at the types of programs available for washing you will come across things that men don't truly understand. Go look at the wash cycle knob and look at the type of cycles that are listed. "Delicate" is a good one. Sure, we know what that probably means but men don't have "delicate' clothes. There are other things listed there but I have no idea what they means and I'm afraid to ask my wife because it will just confirm for her that I wouldn't know what to do without her (and we wouldn't want her to know that, would we?).

WOMEN LIKE TO DO THINGS WITH YOU

Unless your work schedules are completely different, women usually want you to go to bed at the same time they do. Now, I want you to be careful here because this does not mean you're going to have sex. It just means you'll be going to sleep together. When you're coupled, you can no longer use expressions like "going to bed" or "sleeping together" to denote a sexual relationship. Since you'll be going to bed to sleep together every single night, it kind of loses that sexual meaning. I also realize this may be confusing to a manly man because you always equated sleeping together as having sex together. Well my friend, this is just one of the many interesting things you will be learning about women.

Women also like to eat together. Remember how you used to come home, grab a jar of pickles and a pizza and have supper while watching the game? Well that's not going to happen any longer. You'll be eating real food at the table and be expected to participate in some form of checking in at the end of the day. Your woman might also want you to go grocery shopping with her and actually you might want to check this out. At least it increases the likelihood that you'll be getting the chocolate chip cookies you like so much.

WOMEN WATCH YOU

"What's this growing on your arm?" you might hear as your woman starts to look over your skin. This is especially true if you are with someone in the medical profession. Other comments can be, "Are you still biting your nails?", or "If that still itches, you should probably put some lotion on it." If you're not used to someone noticing things about you like this, this can get annoying in a hurry.

THAT SPECIAL TIME OF THE MONTH

If you've never lived around women before then allow me to welcome you to the wonderful world of biology. The female menstrual cycle runs approximately 30 days. The week before a woman ovulates she becomes premenstrual. This can be a very bad time for your woman as serotonin levels in her brain bottom out. If you don't know, serotonin is a neurotransmitter, that is, a chemical that lives in the brain that directly affects mood. And when it goes down, it's not fun. For anyone. You will need to discuss this with your woman (hopefully, not when she's premenstrual) to find out the best way you can support her while she's going through this. If you think this is tough, wait till we get to pregnancy.

By the way, women hate it when every time they're angry at you for something you counter with "What, you getting your period or something?" Try not to do that.

CHAPTER 10

HOW DO YOU KNOW WHEN YOU'RE IN TROUBLE?

As you know by now, being the man means you need to be told everything that is going on emotionally in your relationship. This is especially true when you've done something wrong. The problem here is that there are SO many things that you can do wrong that there's no telling which one of them you did so you can fix it. To make life a bit easier for you, I have dedicated a chapter on how to recognize when there's a problem in your relationship.

So, the number one sign that you're in trouble:

YOUR WOMAN DOESN'T TALK TO YOU!

Remember in earlier chapters when I mentioned how much women enjoy relating ("talking") and how women love to process ("talk")? So, if a woman stops doing something that's so important to her it could only mean one thing: You screwed up royally.

Some other signs include:

YOUR WOMAN DOES NOT MAKE EYE CONTACT.

If your woman is not looking you in the eye then you got problems.

YOUR WOMAN DOES NOT GIVE YOU PHYSICAL CONTACT.

If there is no contact, no touching, no holding hands, no little pats, no contact in any sense of the word, then you're in trouble.

But knowing you're in trouble is only half of it. Your job at this point is to try to figure out what it was you might have done. And she's not going to tell you. But, she will give you clues. And as my patient, Sally, says, "It is the measure of a man to see how long it will take him to notice that his woman is angry at him."

So, let's think together for a minute to see exactly where you might have gone wrong:

Did you mention something about her weight?

Did you forget to notice a new hair style?

Did you insult her in any fashion?

Did you forget to kiss her goodbye, or call her?

Did you mention another woman's name? (Please immediately turn to the chapter "The other woman" if you've done this.

Did you forget a birthday or anniversary or Mother's Day (if appropriate)?

Did you say something about her to her friends or her parents that was not very flattering?

Did you side with one of your family members against her?

Did you not listen to something she was saying?

Did you side with one of the kids in front of her?

Did you not mention marriage? Or commitment?

OK, I give up...I have no idea what she's angry about. You'll have to ask her. But, you'll have to be careful because she may not be ready to tell you.

So, if I were you, I would wait until you are alone and then turn to her and basically throw yourself on the mercy of the court. For example, "Ok, how did I screw up this time?"

If she tells you, at least you're communicating. If she doesn't tell you or basically shakes her head and walks away, it's worse than you thought. You're just going to have to wait until she tells you.

Meanwhile, you may want to start thinking about how you are ever going to make up for whatever it was you did.

CHAPTER 11

THE HARDEST GAME TO PLAY

She sits quietly in the kitchen. Since this is not typical for her, you walk up and say, "What's wrong?"

Her answer? "Nothing."

Now what do you do? Do you ask again? Go away? Get angry?

That's right gentleman, welcome to the hardest game for a man to play in any relationship.

It's the "What's wrong? Nothing" game.

This is a game that starts out long before these words are ever spoken and you don't even know it. It's a game that never has to start but somehow it becomes a key weapon in a woman's arsenal to see if you really care.

The game tends to begin when your woman realizes, through some combination of not listening enough, not paying attention or not being empathetic, that you don't really care.

She might even say those words to you "You don't care!" This will force you to have to convince her that you do care by saying something like, "No sweetie, I really do care. I'm just not good at showing it sometimes."

It actually doesn't matter what you say at this point because your woman already knows you don't really care. And face it guys, you don't.

She wants you to care about the things that hurt her or annoy her or bother her in some way and try as you might, you just can't seem to muster up the level of concern that she would like you to have.

So what's a guy to do?

Simple. Turn to the next chapter and let's see what we can do about keeping you out of trouble.

CHAPTER 12

STAYING OUT OF TROUBLE

Now that you've gone through all this time and effort to get into a relationship, I imagine you'd like to stay in it for a while. So we probably need to go over some of the ways men get themselves into trouble and how they can get themselves out of it. There are certain traps men get themselves into that really get in the way of having a smooth operating relationship. I will list the basic ones.

THE BLAME GAME

There are two basic things you need to know about being in trouble in your relationship,

1) It's your fault.

2) If you're not sure whose fault it is then see #1.

One of the first things we have to change is getting you out of the habit of finding the person to blame. Something went wrong, so it's your fault. You don't have to find out who did what and why. You did it. As long as you are focusing on the problem, you are not focusing on the solution. You will save yourself a lot of time and trouble by focusing on what you need to learn so you don't do whatever it was you did in the first place.

WHO GETS TO WIN

Your relationship is NOT a competitive event. In a healthy relationship there is no "winner" and no "loser". Either both people win or both people lose. It is that simple. This is a team sport...a collaboration. Think of it as being on a doubles team in tennis. You are both standing on the same side of the net. The better you work together, the more things work out for you. When you start competing with your woman over who is right and who is wrong, it is the beginning of the end for the relationship. This brings us to the next trap:

I KNOW WHAT'S RIGHT

This was mentioned in an earlier chapter but it's worth mentioning again. You do not own the truth. You have an opinion and nothing more. And like all opinions they are subject to your own personal biases and your own agenda. If you find yourself in the middle of a conversation in which you are trying to prove to your woman how "right" you are, you can save both of you a lot of time and trouble by stopping what you're doing immediately and regrouping. One other thing you might want to think about; the more you're talking, the less you're listening.

I'M THE KING HERE

This is close to the trap above but it is more about entitlement than what's right. This is the guy who because he works or earns more money or because he's the man or because he sacrificed his beer night or because of a hundred different things, believes he is entitled to special treatment. Guy, you're cruising for a big fall. Get rid of that chip on your shoulder. Nobody owes you anything. You made a decision to bring a woman (and perhaps children) into your life, so live with it. This is your life and you created it. If you don't like it or feel you somehow deserve more, then you may want to talk that one over with your therapist.

EXPECTATIONS

The best way to get disappointed is to have expectations. Here's how it works. You expect a certain thing from your woman but you don't tell her because you expected her to know. She doesn't do it because she didn't know. She didn't know because you didn't tell her. (This works for both sexes equally.) So now you're hurt because she should have known that you wanted this and you shouldn't have had to tell her. So you now resent the fact that she thinks you're wrong for not telling her. You're hurt because you didn't get what you wanted and she's angry because if only you had told her she would have been glad to have given you what you were looking for. We now have two people angry and hurt and no one is getting what they wanted.

DIVISION OF LABOR

For a very simple thing, this gets a lot of men in a lot of trouble. I might have said this earlier but it's worth repeating. Women don't have a special "cleaning" gene that's part of their DNA. Basically, no one loves to clean. It just has to be done and since it also has to be done where you live it might be a good idea if you were to help out. I often suggest couples sit down with each other and draw up a plan for how different jobs around the house are going to get done. The better this works than the better the relationship. As the old saying goes, "A woman never shot a man while he was doing the dishes".

Actually, I have a theory about dirt that I'd like to share. I believe dirt gives off a type of high intensity light that only women can see. This light acts directly on the optic nerve and is very painful to those who can see it (women). For those who cannot see it (men), it offers no discomfort at all. This is why when a man and woman come home from a weekend away and they walk in the front door, the woman looks around as if in pain saying something like, "I can't believe what a pigsty this place is!" The man looks around the same area and sees nothing that disturbs him but he takes her word for it.

FORGETTING

In a relationship there are many things you will be required to remember. It might be a good idea to get used to that right away and figure out how you're going to do this. With all the technology around today, I can't understand why anyone would forget anything, but they do. Here are some of the things that you better remember: birthdays, anniversaries, Christmas, Chanukah, or any other day that deems important enough to remember. And please remember your relationship is not the place where you want to work out your political views. I don't care that you believe Valentine's Day is a plot by the card and flower industry to manipulate the masses with mass purchases of unnecessary products just to get more money out of you. You better show up with a card and a dozen roses.

So, if you are hoping to avoid the situation from the chapter before, try keeping these things in mind. It can really help keep you in a relationship you want to stay in.

CHAPTER 13

ARE WE MARRIED YET?

At some point in your relationship your woman will want to have a "Where is this relationship going?" conversation with you. And you, being the man that you are, will have no absolutely no idea that it's coming. It could start out being just another cozy evening. She's made you a wonderful supper followed by passionate love making. Now you are in "cuddle" position; just laying there, enjoying the closeness of each other's body. Not really saying much.

She will start slowly.

"I think this is my favorite time," she might say as you two enjoy your post-coital embrace.

"Me too," you will respond, because you have no idea of what else to say.

"Oh, did I tell you? Mary Anne is having her engagement party next month" she mentions innocently enough. "And we're invited," she adds as if it was an afterthought.

OK, stop the movie.

Alarms should be going off all through your head. Your internal CPU should be yelling "battle stations" as the little soldier neurons go running through your brain stem, down your spinal column and to the muscles in your legs trying to get them to run as quickly as they can out the door.

But no, you're just lying there calmly, stroking her shoulder noticing how smooth her skin is.

Weren't you listening? Didn't you just hear her say "engagement party"? And you're invited. No, make that "We're" invited. We, as in you and your woman, as in we're a couple and we go places together and everyone knows it including my friend who's having an engagement party next month. You are seen publically as a couple.

But now we wait for the follow-up statement. This will tell you in what direction the conversation is going.

"Let's see", she starts. "I think they've been together ("together", not "seeing each other" not "dating" not "going out" but "together") for just a little bit longer then we have."

Now you're starting to get it, aren't you? A couple getting engaged and she is comparing their timeline to your timeline. Now what do you say? "Oh, that's nice" or "You don't say" or "Cool"?

Yes, my friend, you are going down!

At this point it really doesn't matter what you say. She will be continuing on.

"They both seem so happy", she adds

Do you feel the walls closing in on you? Are the little hairs on the back of your neck standing up now? Or are you just blissfully following the melodic tone of her voice as she leads you down the path of no return.

"Yeh, they do seem happy", you mutter in response.

"Baby?" She asks so shyly as she picks up her head so she can look you straight in the eyes. "When's that going to be us?"

You are dead meat!

You just got asked a question about marriage and it snuck up on you so quietly that you didn't even see it coming. Actually men rarely see anything coming.

So now you have several responses you can choose from depending on these few simple variables:

1) Have you had this conversation before?

2) Are you in your 30's?

3) Is your woman's baby clock ticking?

4) Are you living together?

The more yes's, there are to those questions, the closer you are getting to making a very big decision. So let's go back to your options.

Option 1) "Baby, things are just so right for us the way it is…why rush it?"

Option 1 will only work if this is the first time you've discussed marriage and you've been together under a year and you are in your late 20's (or very early 30's).

Option 2) "I'm sorry honey. What did you just say?

Option 2 will only work if you're mentally defective and English isn't your original language.

Option 3) "You mean (gulp) get married? You want to get married?"

This option will only work if, again, this is the first time you've ever talked about marriage and it inevitably leads to more conversation about marriage.

Option 4) "Honey, I've never really given marriage much thought."

Again, this option only works if this is the first time you've talked about marriage, and it will lead to more conversation about marriage.

Option 5) (And this is the very best option you can take)

"Oh great! You've ruined the surprise! I was going to give you a ring on (pick one, your birthday, Christmas, Valentine's Day)!"

And then you better get your butt to a jewelry store.

If this is not the first time your woman has brought this up and you are still resistant to marrying her then pretty soon you'll be deciding if you want to keep her in your life.

So maybe we should cut to the chase and allow me to help you decide if it's time for you to get married. The following are the top reasons why a man should get married:

1) Your woman will leave you if you don't. You know, you probably don't need anymore reasons than this but just in case you do, I've added a few more.

2) You already do everything together. You see each other every night, talk to each other every day, and spend the entire weekend together. So what's your problem?

3) You or your women want children.

4) She's on your life insurance policy and you're on hers.

5) You can't think of any reason not to marry her.

6) You've lost all ability to live independently

7) She knows you better then you know yourself (and that includes all of your many faults) and she's still willing to put up with you

8) You've become increasingly aware that your days as an adolescent man are coming to an end.

And the last reason why it may now be time for you to get married?

9) Your mother won't take you back.

CHAPTER 14

THE OTHER FAMILY

She finds you sitting in front of the TV (what a surprise). She has paper and pen with her as she places herself next to you on the couch.

"OK", she says. "It's time to work out the holiday schedule."

You look at her. "It's September," you say as if that is some magical spell that will stop her from proceeding.

"Yes it is", she continues. "And if we don't get a start on this now, it's going to be a disaster."

You shut off the TV and turn toward her. You know what's coming because it's been part of your relationship since you have been an official couple. Who will we be spending what holiday with so everyone who has ever been related to either of you will be happy?

If this is your first time trying to figure it all out you will be very surprised as to the power of family traditions. If you are married and have possession of the adored grandchild…watch out!

And so it begins

Welcome to the world of "pleasing the families". This is not a game for the faint of heart. This is no-holds-barred, full-contact choose-your-weapons partnership warfare. It's not so much you versus your woman. It's more like the two of you versus all the combined family members that you two have to deal with. It's also about the level of comfort that you have with the other person's family and how comfortable they are with you.

It is generally around the holidays that these things really heat up.

While some families may have a fondness for the 4th of July or Memorial Day, it's the major holidays that really test the mettle of any family plan. Depending on the proximity of the families, and how crazy everyone is, even the major holidays can be broken up into smaller bits to ensure everyone gets their fair share of their dearly beloved.

Halloween is fairly straightforward. You dress the kid up...you drive the kid to the appropriate front door...you push the doorbell...you yell "trick or treat" as the door opens and family members appear out of the woodwork with cameras and treats and hugs and kisses.

Thanksgiving can be broken down into "dinner" with one family and "dessert" with another. If you happen to live around a major parade area, that can also be a separate part of the day,

Christmas can be broken down into "Christmas Eve", "Christmas morning", "Christmas day, and Christmas dinner"

And let me add one more bit of complication. If either (or both) sets of parents were divorced and remarried then you have one (or more) mother and step-father plus one (or more) father and step mother. I told you this can be tough stuff. Hopefully one of the parents will be Jewish so you'll have someplace to go for Passover and Chanukah. With your luck, your parents will have divorced and both of them will have married a Jewish person so that you now have at least two more holidays to fight over.

But what if your families live out of state and you can't as easily share time with them? That makes things a bit more complicated.

Depending on how far you have to travel, once you are there you are there for the duration. So, there are a few things you may want to discuss before you leave on your thousand mile trip to the land of the Great Unknown.

First, will you be staying with family or will you be getting a hotel room? Will you be depending on family for rides or will you be renting a car? Are you going back to a place where you have friends or are you on your own? Have you worked out a coding system that alerts the other person if you are about to crack?

All these things, and perhaps more, ask two basic questions. 1) How dependent do you want to be on the people you will be with? and 2) What options do you want to give yourselves when you're there.

The answers to these questions depend on how well you can tolerate each other and how sane everyone is. So, regardless of where you are going, or how far you are traveling, there are certain things that will remain true.

If the families are relatively sane and mature then these things are mostly a matter of planning and sharing and taking turns. But add one personality disorder or one hysteric or one depressive to the mix and it can all explode faster then you can say "dysfunctional family".

But this family business is so much more than planning for the holidays. Let me break this down into steps so you'll understand.

STEP 1. MEETING THE FAMILY

How many movies have been made about the significant other meeting his (or her) potential in-laws for the first time? And they each come equipped with their own selection of "characters" that you will have to meet and get along with. There's the disapproving father, the overly intrusive mother, the alcoholic uncle and suicidal aunt, the annoying brother and sister, the stoner cousin, the overly intellectualized brother, and on and on and on. The truth is you will meet some version of all of these people and you will have no idea what to do or how to act. During this process you will be tested and probed so much you will think you've been abducted by aliens.

And it gets worse.

STEP 2. GETTING TO KNOW THE FAMILY

This has three stages to it:

STAGE 1) THE EARLY STAGE

In this stage everyone is still nice to you and to each other. You and they will be on best behavior. No one will be cursing or scratching or being overly provocative. People will apologize if they get inappropriate and will give the impression that they care about you and how you feel (this will change drastically in later stages).

STAGE 2) MID-STAGE

Tempers start to increase a bit as the parents' agenda starts to crystallize. They begin to get frustrated with you if you don't do things the way they would like to see things done. Snide remarks and covert comments will start making their way into the conversation as a way of making sure you know that they don't approve. You start to meet relatives outside of the immediate family. More importantly you are being auditioned for one of several available roles in the family. This leads us to:

STAGE 3) LATE-STAGE

The gloves start to come off a bit more now. The apologies disappear and the comments now come equipped with clearer bits of open hostility thrown in. You start learning more about the family history and current gossip. You get assigned a family role.

THE FAMILY ROLE

You may have read about certain roles that kids end up playing in dysfunctional families and if you have, some of these might sound similar. These roles represent people that the family would like to have for very specific reasons. Most of this is unconscious, so if you're not totally aware of this going on, don't worry about it, neither are they.

The following are assorted roles that may or may not get assigned to you based on your personality, age, strength, success in business and what the family needs:

THE WORKER

As implied, if you become the worker you will never again have nothing to do for the rest of her life. The worker runs errands, chauffeurs other family members around and is basically available on an as your needed basis. And believe me, there is always someone in the family who needs something moved or built or fixed.

THE WISE GUY

Also known as comic relief, this role provides the entertainment for the family. This guy fills in all those nasty silences or distracts from any of the little conflicts that might come up. This role's function is to keep everyone happy. Good luck with that.

PEACE KEEPER

As the name implies, if you take on this role your job will be to make sure all the disagreements are resolved. You will make sure that no one stays angry for very long. Most people who dislike conflict themselves will be drawn to this role because keeping conflict from getting too strong or from happening at all is what this role is all about.

THE INVISIBLE MAN

This is not so much of a role but more like a state of being. If you become this role then no one will ever pay attention to you. They won't ask for your opinion or even notice you when you're around. People will make plans right in front of you without asking for your input. It will become crystal clear that no one wants to hear anything you've got to say.

THE ADVICE GIVER

The opposite of the invisible man, the person in this role, due to their success in business or their profession, will constantly be asked for their advice of what to do. Since you wouldn't be the worker, you wouldn't be expected to do anything more than tell other people what to do.

The trick is, you better be right because if you aren't, you will quickly become the final role of,

THE SCAPEGOAT

If you are this role, you are blamed for everything and I do mean EVERYTHING. In fact, it is the job of this role to take the blame for anything that goes wrong in the relationship, in the family or anywhere in the northern hemisphere. With a scapegoat, at least you'll know whose fault it is.

Depending on the family or the situation or many other variables, roles can be exchanged or not needed or forgotten over time. Keep in mind that the more dysfunctional a family is, the more ridged the roles are.

STEP 3. LIVING WITH THE FAMILY

Now the fun part. You've met them, gotten to know them and now they are in your life. So, here's where it gets tricky. You and your woman will need to work very hard to maintain that delicate balance that exists between the family you are creating and the family that already exists. While you'd like to have a pleasant interface with all family members, you will also want to be able to operate as your own independent family. While this process is going on (and it will take some time), there are a few things to be very, very careful about when getting involved in your woman's family:

Don't make promises you can't keep.

Don't give advice unless you really know what you're talking about.

Never speak poorly about your woman in front of her family.

Don't get too drunk at family functions (you know you're going to say or do something stupid).

Think twice before lending money to family members. You're never going to get it back and you'll end up annoying the other person every time you see him by asking, "Hey, when am I going to get my money back?"

Don't flirt with other family members.

Try to remember everybody's name.

Make sure to compliment the cook.

Suppress all bodily noises and smells at all times.

Try not to make fun of family traditions. They are usually pretty important to the family.

Don't keep secrets from your woman. If someone tells you something and then says not to tell your woman, tell them you are very sorry but you will have to tell her (and then tell her).

Try not to gamble with family members. If you win, you will be resented. If you lose, you will resent them. You'll find enough reasons to resent each other as time goes on. No sense in finding more ways to do that.

If you're visiting and staying with them for some period of time, remember to shower daily.

Also, please keep in mind that when your woman comes to visit with your family, she doesn't know them and they do not know her. She may not want you to disappear on her right away. Wait until they've known each other for awhile. And even then, keep your eyes open, she'll appreciate that.

CHAPTER 15

OTHER WOMEN

This will be a very short chapter because once you are in a committed relationship there are NO other women. Even if you are surrounded by women at work or on the commuter train or grocery store or gym or where ever, THEY DO NOT EXIST!

THERE ARE NO OTHER WOMEN!

THEY ARE A FIGMENT OF YOUR IMAGINATION!

If you happen to make the mistake of mentioning another woman's name to your woman, never, never, never mention that other woman's name again. Since we already know that your woman remembers everything, another woman's name goes into a very special place in her brain and stays there FOREVER!

If you ever make the horrendous and mind-altering mistake of mentioning that women's name again, your women will become very curious as to why you felt the need to talk about her, again. Even if it was 10 years ago, she will remember and she will want to know why you felt the need to mention her again.

So, unless the woman you are mentioning is a nun, a cartoon character, or your sister, please do not mention her name again.

CHAPTER 16

THE AFFAIR

Gentlemen…this is a very important chapter, so please read this very carefully.

I want you to sit down in your favorite, most comfortable chair in your favorite room in the house. I want you to take a deep breath and look around at everything you and your woman have created together. Look at that nice plasma TV on your wall. Think about that refrigerator full of food. Lots of nice things, right?

Still with me? Good.

Now, close your eyes and take a deep breath and imagine that everything you just saw is gone. Imagine yourself living in a studio apartment with a toaster oven for your kitchen. Your nice plasma is now a 13 inch lap top that you found at a yard sale. You get to see your kids (if you have any) every other weekend. The child support comes directly out of your check so you don't have to worry about whether you have it or not.

Having fun yet?

Believe me when I tell you, this is where an affair will lead you.

If you've been paying attention thus far, you have learned a few things; your woman pays attention and knows you better then you know yourself. This means she knows when you are lying to her. I don't care how good a story teller you are or how clever or smart you think you are, she will know that you are lying to her. She doesn't want to believe you would lie to her but that puts her into deep conflict when she thinks you are lying. She will approach you and ask if you've been seeing another woman. You will lie and say no. Part of her knows you are lying but another part of her doesn't want to believe it. Later on, after you admit to everything (and you will end up admitting to everything) she will hate you more for making her crazy than for having the actual affair.

So, if you are thinking about having an affair, I have one piece of advice:

DON'T!

I know it's tempting. She laughs at your jokes (the way your woman used to: before she heard them 500 times). She pays attention to you the way your woman used to. She touches you in that oh, so, seductive way. She shares her problems with you and asks for your advice. She makes you feel important (the way you used to feel with your woman).

She is probably younger, which means she looks up to you and values what you say to her and (here's the really important part) SHE DOESN'T CARE THAT YOU'RE MARRIED.

This is a really important clue for you because what I know about most women is, they care if you're married or not.

Affairs are like going to Disney World. Nothing is real but you don't care because you're having such a great time.

When you are in an affair, it's like creating a bubble around you. All the pressures and stressors and problems of your everyday world disappear. The only thing that matters is the total pleasure you get from being with someone who thinks you're the greatest thing since sliced bread.

It is like a drug…very powerful and quite addictive.

So, if you find yourself attracted to a woman outside of your relationship, before you do anything, sit down and think through what this actually means to you.

For example, if you really like it when she tells you how you really understand her more then anyone she's met in a long time and she thanks you for every little thing you do for her and tells you how she really looks forward to when she's going to see you again, you may want to stop and think about how strongly you need to have these things from a woman. And then you think about when the last time was that you felt this from your wife.

Once you realize that you've been missing this in your relationship, you go home and have a heart-to-heart conversation with your woman about how much you miss those times when she made you feel so important and so needed. And how much you'd like to get that back. You may be surprised to find out she's been missing the exact same thing.

Then you plan a day or an afternoon or a weekend (whatever you can do) with just the two of you and you get started on finding what it was that started to get away from you. Now, you get to keep your house and your car and you might even end up with a better relationship as well.

CHAPTER 17

SERIOUS PROBLEMS

Every couple goes through their ups and downs. It's the nature of relationships. What you want to do is to have enough emotional equity in the relationship bank so when you need to make a withdrawal, it is there.

This chapter is about something quite different. It is perhaps the most serious of the chapters because it deals with those things that can end up destroying a relationship or even worse, destroying a family. Most of these things occur over time and unless you're really paying attention, by the time you realize what's going on it's often too late.

Let's start with the number one reason why relationships stop working:

THE EROSION OF INTIMACY

This sound pretty ominous but what exactly does it mean?

Let's start with the concept of erosion. I'm sure you're familiar with that. It's the ocean running up against the shore; day after day, year after year. The ocean pounds away as bit by bit, the sand breaks free and washes back into the sea. Every so often there's a huge storm and large chunks of dirt and rock disappear. A shore line can only stand a number of these storms before the shape of the entire coastline is changed forever. But mostly it's the day by day action of the water against the land that creates the erosion.

This is very similar to what can happen to a relationship if two people are not paying attention to the emotional waves that are crashing around them.

Now let's look at intimacy.

This may be a harder concept for you. It implies vulnerability and openness. These are typically NOT manly concepts but are necessary in a healthy relationship. You've heard the word a lot and may have some sense as to what it is and how it's supposed to work, but for our purposes let me clarify.

Intimacy is the glue that holds a relationship together.

Trust and communication are its main ingredients. Should one of these ingredients fail and the intimacy starts to erode then the relationship will start to fall apart. It may not end at this point but it will certainly be wounded and will need to be nursed back to health. The "storm" I mentioned is the yelling and screaming that can signify that the relationship is hurting and needs quick repair.

By the time you get to this point, there are probably several things that have occurred that need your attention;

BROKEN TRUST

Trust is the easiest thing to break and hardest thing to repair. It occurs when you start either lying to your woman or you stop paying attention to her. It occurs when your woman finds it harder and harder to believe you because of all the broken promises you've made. Every time you're later than you said you would be or you don't show up at all or you don't take your woman's concerns seriously or try to joke your way out of a serious situation, you lose a bit of credibility. This makes it harder for your woman to trust you. Unless this stops, the mistrust will build to the point where your woman will not believe anything you tell her. This is the beginning of the end of a relationship.

DEFENSIVENESS

What are defenses? They are psychological devices designed to protect you from psychological harm. Some of them include denial, projection, minimization, deflection, displacement, justification, etc, etc. We all use them because we all want to think we're good people. Unfortunately the more "bad" we do, the more we need defenses to keep ourselves from realizing that we're actually doing bad things to people we're suppose to love. Denial is probably the first of the defenses we learn.

Imagine you're sitting in your living room and you hear a crash coming from the kitchen. You run in to find your three-year-old with a cookie in her hand and bits of cookie jar all over the floor. As soon as she sees you, what's the first thing she says? "I didn't do it." If you ask her what happened she might even come up with a story about how. "Uh…this big dog came in and…uh…jumped on the counter and…uh…knocked over the cookie jar". And she would be so happy with the story she came up with that she would be smiling and happy at the end of it. Why the denial? Simple. If she was the kind of little girl who knocked over cookie jars, then she would be "bad" and would have to be punished. The story was her proof that she didn't do anything to deserve punishment (and she will even believe it). So what does this have to do with you?

Let's say you come home from work very late and you didn't call and there's alcohol on your breath. You walk in the door and there is your woman waiting for you. At first she's relieved because you're alive but her next thought is she wants to be the one to kill you. What do you say when she tells you you're home awfully late? You say something like, "Not really." (Denial, the little girl and the cookie jar). Or you might say, "It's really not that late" (minimization) or you might begin with a story about how one of your coworkers was leaving and you went out after work for a quick, goodbye drink and the next thing you knew it was one in the morning and you knew you had to get home. So, being the loving man that you are, you left early just so you wouldn't be home too late. Now this is clearly a justification with a twist of an ending. You're trying to make it sound like you're really a good guy for coming home when you did because it could have been much later. Or the other response you could have had was, "You know, you stay out late sometimes to." This is deflection. You're trying to get the attention off of you and on to her.

All of these defenses are designed to protect you. What they end up doing is getting in the way of good honest communication. Your woman knows you're making this up as you go along. It's usually best just to say you're sorry and make sure it doesn't happen again.

By the way, apologies only go so far. If you're really good at apologizing, it means you've had to do it often. At some point apologies are meaningless unless you're changing your behavior.

AUTOMATIC COMMUNICATION

This is basically an interaction that resembles communication but is really not. It's a style of talking to each other that evolved over time and is generally quite harmful to the relationship because it keeps you from learning new and healthier ways to talk to each other. It combines elements of defensiveness, mistrust and emotional distance. It sounds something like this:

"What time did you get home last night?"

"What do you care, you were sleeping."

"You never call me anymore to let me know what you're doing."

"Well, things come up that I have to take care of."

"And you couldn't call to let me know?"

"Why, so you could yell at me about not coming home, again? You know I'm getting pretty tired of that."

"Well, maybe if you were around more often or spent time with your family or didn't disappear all night long then maybe I wouldn't be yelling at you. Did you ever think of that?"

"There you go again. It's always my fault isn't it? But you're perfect. You never do anything wrong. It's always me."

OK, I don't think we need to hear any more of that. That, my friend, is what I call emotional fencing and it's automatic. Neither one of these people is thinking about what they're saying. They're just expressing levels of emotion (mostly hostility). And this can get much worse and much louder and can easily disintegrate into name calling, insulting and threatening.

It's not a pretty sight.

In couple's work, whenever you see this going on (and it pretty much happens right away) your first job is to see if you can get people to talk to each other in a respectful way. If you can't, then that is usually the end of the relationship.

ERRORS IN COMMUNICATION

This is similar to the preceding section but a bit different. These are the things both men and woman do that interfere with good, healthy communication (so, you're slightly off the hook, it's not just men). They include the following:

ASSUMPTIONS

As the name implies, this is when one person assumes they know what the other person means or what they're thinking or feeling without checking it out. No matter how smart or intuitive you are or how long you've been together I always ask people to check out what they think is going on before they assume it is the truth (As I was taught in US Air Force many, many years ago, when you "assume" something you make an "ass" out of "u" and "me".) Get it? Ass out of u and me? Never mind…

MIND READING

Very similar to assumptions in that you believe you know what your partner is thinking or feeling without asking.

TELLING…NOT ASKING

This follows one of the two proceeding sections above. Once you believe you know what is going on and think it is the truth, you now start telling your partner what she is thinking or feeling (instead of asking). Now she had to correct you but you don't believe her because you think you know the truth. And this little game can go on and on and nobody wins.

ABUSIVE BEHAVIORS

When these types of behaviors are exhibited it calls for immediate action and probably should lead to couple's counseling or in some cases, police involvement.

INTIMIDATION

This includes yelling, threatening, physically imposing yourself over someone, taking something out of someone's hand (a phone?) or in any way possible trying to force your will over your woman's. This is dangerous and could easily lead to the next step.

PHYSICAL ACTION

No man should ever put his hands on a woman when it is not invited. No man should ever strike a woman, ever. You should not prevent a woman from leaving a room, or the house or try to keep her from protecting herself. If you find yourself wanting to hurt your woman (for whatever reason), leave and don't come back until you are under control.

ABUSE OF ALCOHOL OR DRUGS

This is tricky. I could have easily written a book solely on this area but I want to keep it simple. There is a saying, "The alcoholic is the last to know." If you are overdrinking or using drugs you probably feel there is nothing wrong with what you are doing and you might be right.

However, the early signs of alcohol and drug abuse are fairly subtle and require close scrutiny. You might think that a man with alcohol or drug problems is probably sleeping under a bridge at night and begging for money during the day. This describes a very small percentage of people with substance abuse issues. Most abusers or alcoholics generally function pretty well. They have homes and children and jobs. What they are starting to lose, however, is the emotional closeness with their family.

As you sit in the evening and have your nightly cocktail, beer or herb, it pulls you emotionally away from the people around you. Did you ever try to have serious conversation with someone who is stoned or under the influence of alcohol and you're not? Try it sometime and let me know how it goes. Because this is the same feeling your woman has about you if you are a heavy user of substances.

GAMBLING

Like the use of substances, there is gambling and there is GAMBLING! An occasional card game, scratch ticket, game day card, horse race, etc, etc, could turn out to be a fun time if you are betting within limits and not exceeding what you set as a limit for yourself. Then there are those who keep gambling until they lose everything. Don't let that be you.

PORN

Another tricky one. Pornography is generally, but not always, a man's activity. Most women that I know consider it demeaning and insulting to women everywhere. Most men find it to be exciting and inviting. Many an evening has been wasted while a man peruses the Internet looking for the best in porn. Here, the acceptability of this depends on the relationship, how well the activity is hidden from others (children) and how this affects a man's relationship with real women. Most men can enjoy brief forays into porn and then pull themselves out fairly quickly. Others find it far too addicting and end up believing that these are somehow real relationships they are having.

CHAT LINES

This is porn in real life. This is when you happen to be on the Internet and just happen to strike up a little online conversation with a woman you never met. The conversation evolves to the point where you might even arrange for an in-person meeting and that meeting might even happen. And then one fateful day your woman discovers that you've been involved with another woman. You will argue that it never got to be physical so it's not officially "cheating". Your woman will counter with the notion that it doesn't have to get physical to be cheating. There is such a things as "emotional cheating" and you've been doing it.

GETTING HELP

If you believe you are having problems in these areas or if your woman has pointed out her concerns in one of these areas, then it may be time to get some help. Help can come in many different forms. You can speak to your priest, minister or rabbi. You could talk to a friend, parent, teacher, coach, employee assistance program (EAP) provider, doctor, psychiatrist or therapist. You can pick up some books on the subject. You can go online and research the concern. There are so many ways to get information and find resources that the worst thing you can do is nothing.

In fact, after 30 years or so of doing couple's work, there is one theme that occurs over and over again. Couples wait too long to get help. Quite often by the time they get to me, there is so much pain and anger and resentment that there is very little left for me to do except help them plan their divorce.

The longer you wait, the harder it gets.

I know it's not manly to ask for help (forget about asking for directions). But is it manlier to watch your relationship go down the tubes and do nothing about it?

By the way, if your woman thinks there's a problem…there's a problem.

CHAPTER 18

SEX

"A man will listen to anything if he thinks it's foreplay."

Susan Sarandon in Bull Durham

So what can I say about sex that you don't already know?

-You know men and women typically have different levels of sexual urges.

-You know that men and women have sex for different reasons.

-You know that sexual urges change, for both men and women, over time.

You also know that sexual performance can be an important identifier for men. If a man believes he cannot perform well sexually, it will affect his self esteem and his willingness to take chances in relationships. If a woman believes she is not a desirable sexual partner it will affect her self esteem and her willingness to take chances in relationships.

So how did sex get to be so important?

Two words: biology and culture.

But I know you don't want a lecture on biology and culture so instead, let's cut to the chase:

How do you get more sex in your relationship?

First of all, if you approach sex as a separate behavior apart from the rest of your relationship, you will be in trouble. A good sexual relationship generally means a good relationship. If things are going wrong in one aspect of the relationship it will tend to get played out in the bedroom.

If sex becomes another expression of your closeness, then you might end up having more sex. If that's your goal, then please keep these simple rules in mind:

1) Foreplay begins at 7 AM not 7 PM. Showing your woman that you are interested in her throughout the day and not when you just want to jump her bones might actually convince her that you care about her.

2) Listen to your woman and she will give you clues as to what you can expect from her. When your woman says things like, "I'm really tired" or "Work was really stressful today" or "I've haven't been feeling so good", you won't be getting any. But that doesn't mean you just disappear into your video game. You offer comfort and support. It takes a real man to "cuddle" with no expectation of sex.

3) Establish a healthy way for you and your woman to clearly and effectively communicate about all your needs, not just the sexual ones.

4) Make sex more fun and satisfying for both of you. If sex is pleasurable for you and you alone, then your woman will not be quite as excited about the prospect of having sex with you. But, if she's having fun too…well, that's a different story, isn't it?

5) Keep desire alive. Stay in good physical shape and encourage your woman to do the same. Healthier people tend to be more comfortable with their bodies and therefore feel sexier.

CHAPTER 19

YOU MEAN YOU'RE STILL MAD AT HER?

You have got to be kidding me, right?

So what did she do? Make you wait? Spend too much money on something? Make a decision about something you didn't like? Said "no"?

What was it that got you so angry?

So how long do you plan on punishing her? Want to yell a bit more? Call her names? Whatever it was just keep in mind, the longer you stay mad at her the more payback you'll get when you screw up. And believe me, some time down the road, you will screw up

Here are a couple of things I'd like you to keep in mind:

1) Nobody is perfect. Everyone makes mistakes (which is why they put erasers on pencils). Mistakes are part of the learning process. Our mistakes often teach us more than our success. Do not expect perfection from yourself or your woman or anyone in the world. It will not happen and you will end up disappointed and angry.

2) Forgiveness is the acknowledgement that we all make mistakes. You like to be forgiven when you mess up and so do others. Your woman is no different.

3) If you do not forgive, then you are doomed to carry the weight of resentment with you until you do. As the saying goes, "Resentment is like taking poison and waiting for the other person to die."

4) Forgiveness is not about freeing up someone else; it's about freeing you up so you don't have to carry the weight of your anger around with you.

So, if after all this you feel like you still have to be angry at your woman, go right ahead. Just keep in mind, what comes around, goes around. And believe me, there will be a next time for you as well.

CHAPTER 20

BECOMNG A PARENT

If your relationship has survived this long, then you may be discussing the notion of bringing children into the world. Then again, you may be trying to come up with reasons why you SHOULDN'T bring children into the world.

Either way there are three fundamental truths you may want to consider:

1) You can never know how it feels to be a parent until you are a parent.

2) It is never a good time to have a child.

3) You can never know what it's like to live with a pregnant woman until you've lived with a pregnant woman.

GETTING PREGNANT

Step one in becoming a parent (following all those conversations about whether you should or you shouldn't or can or can't or when or how or all the millions of questions and concerns that people have about having a baby): Basically, there is really only one reason why anyone has a baby...they want to.

This is also the only time when a man finally gets the amount of sex he always wanted. And sometimes he ends up getting a lot more sex then he ever wanted and in ways that don't quite fit the fantasy. You know how the fantasy goes, don't you? It's about seduction…about having power over a woman in ways that she cannot resist you.

It is definitely NOT about coming home from work, walking in the front door of your abode and having your woman grab you by the shirt and mention to you in the most intense of manners, "We have to have sex now!"

Then, without even waiting for an answer, she drags you into your bedroom where she takes your clothes off, throws you onto the bed and as she undresses, tells you exactly what position you need to be in and for how long.

At this point you have now basically become… SPERM ON DEMAND!

No time for seduction scenes, foreplay or even worrying about orgasms. Just get that thing in there, shake it around and make the delivery.

Never has a sexual encounter been brought to its most basic details.

Most men might even enjoy this the first or even the second time around for those special five to seven days a month when the little eggs are in there somewhere waiting for the little spermies to come swimming along. But sex on demand gets old after a while and soon men are reduced to having second thoughts about coming home.

But not to worry, this period of time is designed to help you get over the fact that once your woman gets ready to deliver your baby, you won't be having sex for quite some time. So, enjoy it while you got it.

Then, after consulting the moon charts, the I Ching, your astrological forecast, your local psychic, energy reader or psychotherapist, you are finally pregnant.

Here, I would like to pause a moment and say a brief word to those couples who try and try and try and cannot get pregnant. I am really sorry. This does not mean you are bad people or that God doesn't want you to have children. It just means the biology is not right and for that my heart goes out to you. Fortunately, there are so many infants and children out there that need a home and loving parents that everything you have to offer as good, loving people will not go to waste.

But to the people who can and do get pregnant. It's time for the next stage of parenting...

BEING PREGNANT

These 40 weeks or so are nature's way of getting you ready for your life to change in profound and unpredictable ways. The things that are happening to your woman's body as her pregnancy progresses are not only strange and miraculous but downright uncomfortable.

As the weeks go by and the fetus gets larger (i.e. takes up more room inside your woman's body), things get very interesting. (By the way, "interesting" is a word that you can use only if the thing mentioned is not happening to you.)

Your woman's bladder ends up the size of a walnut meaning she will have to use the bathroom every ten minutes. Her body temperature will go up to about 200 degrees Fahrenheit (which makes pregnancy during the heart of the summer really fun).The extra 20 to 40 pounds that she will tack on will mean the end of sleep as she knows it. Try tying a watermelon around your waist and then see how well you sleep. Her kidneys will be pushed into her liver and her lungs will end up shoved into her stomach, which is now a third of the size it once was. This means she has to eat continuously through out the day. Don't get me started about what happens to her intestines.

Now the hormones. These are very powerful chemicals that are surging through your woman's body. These very same chemicals also tend to affect mood, leading to a wide range of emotions throughout the pregnancy.

And you, my friend, you will have the great opportunity to live through this with your woman and support her as she goes through all this biological upheaval. You may get woken up at night with her staring at you. "I can't sleep," she might wish to share with you at that time. Then there's the ever popular midnight run to your local 24-hour convenience store so you can pick up the pickles or ice cream or grape jelly or whatever it is she has to have that instant.

You will learn about all these things in baby class because everyone goes to baby class. While baby class is full of good information and a great way to meet other couples who are also getting ready to have a baby, it is mostly serves the purpose of giving the man something to do while his woman is going to be delivering a child. We get to "coach" our women through the delivery process. This will be little consolation to your woman as she is trying to push a six to twelve pound living thing through her vagina. And there is that really special time during delivery when your woman grabs you by the throat and yells at the top of her lungs, "YOU DID THIS TO ME!"

But I'm getting ahead of myself. We now come to the day of delivery. This is the time when your woman casually announces to you that her water has broken and she believes she is getting ready to deliver. Or she might be experiencing some labor pains and wakes you up to let you know, "It's time." You will look at her confused asking, "It's time for what?" She will smile and say, "The baby is getting ready to come out." You will repeat that to yourself, "The baby is getting ready to come out…the baby is getting…." Now suddenly the adrenaline starts to flow through your body. You will look at her as though she just told you the rocket ship is ready to take you to Mars.

Let's stop the movie here for a second and allow me to share with you a theory I have about men. While during the past 9 months or so, the man has recognized that his woman was getting bigger, and intellectually he knew there was probably a good reason for that, he didn't emotionally know why until his woman tells him she is ready to deliver. And now, as if he's realizing it for the first time, the knowledge that his woman is about to deliver his baby goes up the cerebral cortex into the frontal lobe area where it engages the thought patterns necessary to crank up the adrenal glands…and he is off and running.

He will now be running around all over the place making sure everything is in order. Who he has to call, what he has to do, get the car, get to the hospital, no, make sure he has his woman with him and now, get to the hospital. The woman, fortunately, will already have her bag packed with everything she will need and will be sitting patiently while she watches her man run around like an insane chicken. ("Insane chicken." Good name for a rock group.)

Now, you, the attentive and comforting man, are by your woman's side as she pushes this baby out of her. Before you know it, you will be in total shock as you watch a baby come out of your wife's body. For those couples who choose or who have to have a C section, The experience is slightly different but intense none the less.

At the end of it all, you, your woman and your new baby will be together in the hospital room or birthing room or taxi cab or whereever you managed to be when the baby came.

Welcome to the beginning of parenthood.

BEING A PARENT

Guys, here's where things get tricky. Your job is about to change drastically and I certainly hope you're ready for it because ready or not, it's here.

Your woman and your baby form a perfect biological circle…like a leaf and a tree…they are connected through an incredible link that has connected mother and child from the beginning of civilization. This is a connection that you will not be able to experience in quite the same way but that doesn't matter right now.

The first thing that you need to deal with is that you are no longer your wife's little boy. You will no longer get the affection and attention you once did in the way you did it. Your new baby now occupies that space. It is time for you to, as they say, "man up".

You may no longer be the little boy because they now need the man. You have been promoted to warrior.

Your job is now to protect, defend and secure the space where mother and child bond. This is your link back to men of a hundred generations ago. This is your responsibility now.

Now some men may have issues with this. They may feel ignored or slighted or diminished in some way. To those men I say to you that your job has never been more important. Your woman and your new baby need you. They depend on you now more then they ever have.

You may feel left out at first but that will change. As the first few months go by and symbiosis between mother and child lessens a bit, you will start to be included more in the daily routine of child care. You will, you lucky guy, be changing diapers before you know it. And like all things you do, you will become a master diaper changer. And the more time that goes by, the more opportunities you will have to be connected to your baby.

At times it may be hard for you to remember but this is a life that you have helped create and it will learn from you, the teacher, how to deal with the world.

You are now a father.

I could go on and on about parenthood and raising kids but that's not what this book is really about. So I suggest you focus on the relationship with your woman and wait for my next book to come out, "A Child's Guide to Parents."

Then we can talk.

POST SCRIPT

I need to thank so many people and so many couples that I have seen over the years of my practice that it would be impossible to mention everyone.

To my coworkers and colleagues who gave me feedback, chapter by chapter, I thank you so much.

To the couples who have worked with me, you may recognize pieces of yourselves and your relationships in this book. Thank you for all that you have taught me.

To my wife: As always, I am so thankful to you for putting up with me and for supporting me in our life and its many challenges. For, as we both know, I am just a lowly man and could not have made it without you in my life.

To my children: Laura, Scott and Rachel...I have mentioned your names so now you have to read the book.